— *the* —
MARRIAGE
Dance

Practice the Steps

the MARRIAGE *Dance*

Practice the Steps

Bob and Roxann Andersen

Gentle Impact Publishing
6185 Magnolia Avenue #350
Riverside, CA 92506

ISBN 978-0-9907259-2-3

Cover Photo by Amy Veen Frazier
Cover Design by Frazier Media
Interior Design by *k*ae Creative Solutions

Published in the United States of America.

Published by
Gentle Impact Publishing
6185 Magnolia Avenue #350
Riverside, CA 92506

Dedication

This book is for the "marriage dancers" who are willing to practice the steps, sweat, and endure a few bruises—and endure some pain—in order to enjoy a beautiful, passionate marriage the way God designed it to be.

Table of Contents

Foreword

When we published The Marriage Dance, we thought we were done. We are glad God didn't tell us then that we would be writing a workbook. After giving a number of seminars, we discovered we could give couples good ideas and new insights in a day or two. However, it was not possible for them to implement those ideas in that time frame.

We set out to dissect the original book in order to allow each couple to dedicate the necessary time to think, talk, and pray through each concept. In particular, the areas of sins and wounds take a while to digest. We hope you will take the necessary time to ponder and pray through whatever puts roadblocks in your relationship. As you do, we pray God will give you a deeper, smoother, more passionate marriage than you ever dreamed possible.

Acknowledgments

We want to thank those who have been instrumental to the creation of this workbook:

- Mike Pierpoint for cheering us on and providing a test venue at every leg of the journey.

- Peggy Muller who helped draft thoughtful questions that made the principles applicable.

- Deryl and Brenda Lackey who gave us the idea of "keeping the conversation going."

- The members of our Sunday School class and Kathy Posegate's Bible study who have prayed for us day by day.

- Our mentor couples: Charlie and Gayle Thorne, Dave and Vickie Cochrane, and Jonathan and Terri Kane who shared their lives, their stories, and their love with their table groups.

- The couples who comprised the pilot groups for the studies: Marcus and Stephanie Vigil, Don and Cathy Welton, Dave and April Smith, Richard and Dee Perez, Eric and Elina Gonzalez, Charles and Jingmei Ruggles, Eric and Cynthia Salveson—and especially the three couples who were serious enough about their marriages to go through the workshop twice: Aaron and Amber Bernreuter, Marvin and Angelica Powell, and Jason and Janeen Shafer.

Introduction

How to use the Practice-the-Steps Guidebook

This study is based on the book *The Marriage Dance: Moving Together as One*. While there is a summary at the beginning of each session, participants will get a fuller understanding if they read the entire chapter in the book.

Summaries are followed by a section entitled, "Improve Your Technique." This section is designed for individual Bible study, meditation, and prayer. In ballroom dance, becoming a proficient dancer requires working on your own technique first. Individuals should allow 30-60 minutes per week to complete the "Improve Your Technique" sections.

Next each individual should answer the questions in "Private Lesson." Then the couple should review the answers with your mate. "Private Lesson" allows couples to think through the topic and share their insights with each other. Allow 30-60 minutes. Don't shortchange this time together.

"Group Class" takes place during the weekly meeting. The term refers to ballroom dance lessons given in a group setting as opposed to a private lesson. It is an opportunity to learn from others. Form groups of four to five couples. After the first couple of weeks, the groups should remain fixed. Allow 30-60 minutes for discussion, sharing prayer requests, and praying.

"Practice the Steps" is a place for you to list your insights and goals each week.

Throughout the book you will find "Bonus" sessions. We urge you to join in enthusiastically so you can become a wonderful marriage partner.

A leader's guide can be found at the back of the book.

Small Group Covenant

Joining a group is a sacred commitment. The group members depend on you to attend group sessions, participate with enthusiasm and openness. Review the covenant below and sign your name indicating your pledge to join and share in your *Practice-the-Steps* small group.

Covenant

I will do my best to …

- Be on time.

- Give priority to this group by doing the homework and attending unless there is a circumstance beyond my control.

- Participate openly and honestly in group sessions, giving my best input, but also giving opportunity for all group members to share.

- I will not share what someone said inside the group unless I have the person's specific and express permission to do so.

_____

Signature

_____

Date

Guidelines for Group Prayer

- I will be prepared to share how the group can support me in prayer.
- I will be brief and personal.
- I understand that it is not necessary for me to pray aloud.
- I will pray for other group members at my table.

Suggested 12-Week Schedule

DATE	WORKBOOK SESSION	*THE MARRIAGE DANCE* CHAPTER COVERED IN THE SESSION
	1	1~Metaphor of The Marriage Dance 2~Embrace Your Differences
	2	3~Do You Want to Dance? 4~Connect the Partners
	3	5~Lead with Confidence
	4	6~Follow with Strength
	5	7A~Sins (Bitterness)
	6	7B~Sins (Pride)
	7	7C~Sins (Rebellion, Craving Things that Don't Last, Sexual Sins, Hypocrisy)
	8	8~Wounds: Everyone is Wounded
	9	9~Wounds: Beware Your Reaction
	10	10~Wounds: Resolution of Wounds
	10 Bonus	Bonus~Help Your Partner Resolve His or Her Wounds
	11	11~The Winning Couple
	12	12~The Ultimate Marriage Dance

The Metaphor of *The Marriage Dance* and Embrace Your Differences

The Metaphor of the Marriage Dance

Chapter 1, pages 11-16 from *The Marriage Dance*
For a better understanding of this topic, we suggest you read the full chapter.

Marriage is like a dance, and because we are different people, we must discover our roles in the structure and beauty of that dance. One partner leads and the other agrees to follow. Both must be competent in fulfilling their parts. Neither is superior; neither is inferior. Obstacles get in the way of a harmonious relationship. In dance, obstacles may be bad habits or areas where further skill must be developed. In marriage, the unresolved sins and wounds from our past are often the culprits that repeatedly trip us. In either case, we have to go back and get them right before we can dance beautifully together. The payoff for competitive dancers who work consistently and diligently toward their goal is winning a big trophy. The payoff for a husband and wife who are willing to keep "honing their craft" is far greater. It's a marriage that glides harmoniously, enjoyably, and passionately the way God intended it to.

Embrace Your Differences

Chapter 2 pages 17-27 from *The Marriage Dance*
For a better understanding of this topic, we suggest you read the full chapter.

Embrace Your Differences

God designed a husband and wife to be different from each other. When God created a helper "suitable" for Adam in Genesis 2:18, He made her a complement—not a carbon copy. If the two of you insist on acting and behaving the same, the dance becomes a competition. Accepting and using your differences to your advantage makes you stronger. Whether your differences are a stumbling block or a benefit is a matter of perspective, acceptance, and harmony.

Life Experiences

We enter marriage with certain assumptions based on our prior life experiences. We may not think to express our rules because we may not recognize them ourselves. These unspoken assumptions can turn into conflict. Each couple must decide whether different life experiences and different outlooks will create obstacles or become tools to build a more powerful team. For example, consider a scenario like this: One spouse was raised in a home where money was handled carefully and spent prudently, and the other spouse was raised in a home where money was plentiful. How could these life experiences give rise to unspoken assumptions that cause problems?

Gender
While society blurs the distinctions between the genders, ballroom dance celebrates them. Each gender is needed for a beautiful dance. The men almost blend into the background in dance. They provide structure. The ladies are there to dazzle.

Dr. John Gray, famous for his book *Men are from Mars and Women are from Venus* also wrote *When Mars and Venus Collide.* He points out that men tend to prioritize their problems and work toward "fixing" them as quickly as possible. Women, would rather connect with another human being and talk the problem through to a solution. Often, the two methods are in conflict and cause conflict. Gray also asserts that hormonal differences affect how the genders react to stress, dangerous situations, and sex. Is one method superior and the other inferior? We don't think so. Rather, an acceptance of and respect for both makes a couple a stronger team.

Personality

Do you and your spouse have different personalities? The odds are you do. And people with different personalities often get on each other's nerves or the more dominant personality type will try to use those personality differences to his or her advantage. The Let's-Party gal marries Steady-Eddy because deep down she knows she needs a steadying influence. The fast-charging Git-r-done partner marries someone who is good at taking care of details because he or she needs balance. Then, Let's-Party gets frustrated because Steady-Eddy is sedentary. Git-r-done gets angry at how long it takes to get the details right. Accepting personality differences and learning the value of your partner's traits is a positive and completing force in your marriage.

If you focus on how your differences can help you work together as a team, you will create a highly functioning unit for the glory of God's Kingdom.

For a more complete treatment of this subject, read *The Marriage Dance* by Bob and Roxann Andersen, Chapter 2, "Embrace Your Differences."

Improve Your Technique

After reading the summary above (or the entire chapter in *The Marriage* Dance) complete the questions below. This section should take you less than an hour to complete. We recommend you complete the <u>Improve Your Technique</u> section alone before completing the <u>Private Lesson</u> section with your spouse. The <u>Group Class</u> section will be completed in your small group.

Read Genesis 2:18. Why do you think God said it is not good for a man to be alone?

What are your initial thoughts on what it means to be a "suitable" helper?

Think of your favorite sports team, musical group, or the team of people you work with. What makes them good teammates?

When the team doesn't work well together, what causes it?

If one person on the team thinks that he or she is the best team member on the team, how does that attitude impact the team?

If you think of yourself as better than your spouse (not just in a particular area, but overall), how will that attitude affect your marriage?

Ask God to shine His light on any thoughts of superiority in you. Write what He reveals in the space below.

If you feel inferior to your spouse, how will that attitude affect the team?

Ask God to reveal the truth about whether you are inferior. (If you need help in this area, read Galatians 3:28 and Jeremiah 1:5.)

Ask God to show you the particular and specific areas or ways that you behave because of less-than-favorable traits in you. Record them in the space below.

Read 1 Timothy 1:15. Did Christ accept you despite your flaws?

Read Romans 15:7. How should you treat your spouse's less-than-favorable qualities?

Does your spouse help make you better in these areas? How?

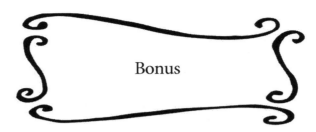

Bonus

Read I Corinthians 12:4-30. The passage is a discussion of how people with different spiritual gifts should work together in the body of Christ. However, these principles are helpful for any group—or couple—trying to work together.

According to this passage, which team member is the most important? What do you think is God's purpose for giving different gifts?

God gave different spiritual gifts within the body of Christ. Do you think He was caught unaware that these differences would cause tension? If not, why did He do it?

Read Romans 12. In your words, describe the actions and principles that will help you be a better teammate in the body of Christ. Put a check mark by the ones that also apply to marriage.

Private Lesson

Ask God to direct your discussion to the areas and issues you need to discuss.

After answering these questions on your own, set aside uninterrupted time together to discuss your answers—a quiet date night would be perfect. If possible, discuss these questions after you have completed the <u>Improve Your Technique</u> exercises.

How well would you say that you and your spouse function together as teammates? Rate yourself on a scale of 1-10.

Need Work 1   2   3   4   5   6   7   8   9   10 Exceptionally Good Teammates

Did you agree with your spouse's evaluation? Why or why not?

On the chart below, list your differences.

Husband	Wife
Life Experiences (e.g. raised in a different country, strict upbringing versus latch key kid)	
Gender (e.g. differences caused by hormones, priorities, reactions)	
Personality (e.g. dominant, intuitive, happy-go-lucky, thinker, fast-paced)	

What other differences affect your marriage? How do they cause friction? How do they cause joy?

What quality first attracted you to your spouse?

Why was that quality so attractive to you?

Do you think you were drawn to your spouse because that quality complemented you?

List some areas in which you work well together.

List areas that repeatedly cause tension. How might they be turned into a strength?

Have you turned any differences into strengths in the past? If so, how did you do it?

List the qualities you appreciate in your spouse. Include specific gifts and insights as well as the spice he or she adds to your marriage. Be specific.

1. _____

2. _____

3. _____

4. _____

5. _____

List the qualities that are not appreciated by each spouse. Beside each one, write how you can view that negative as humorous rather than irritating.

As a couple, determine a new mindset that you are on the same team and want to move together skillfully and harmoniously. Be honest and prayerful as you make this commitment together. What is your next step to move together as one?

Ask God to help you resolve any problem areas.

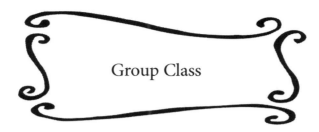

Group Class

Before we begin, introduce yourselves to the group.

- How long have you been married?
- How did you meet?
- What are some of your spouse's best qualities?

Your mentor couple will lead your small group in discussing these questions. If you do not want to share, it is perfectly okay to pass.

1. What are some of the differences between you and your spouse?

2. Did anyone have an example of differences that made you laugh?

3. Share something you discovered that you and your spouse do better because you are a team.

4. What were your biggest "ah-ha" moments regarding embracing your differences as a couple and committing to being on the same team?

5. How would you treat your spouse differently if you viewed them as a teammate than if you did not?

6. How can you encourage your marriage teammate to be the best player they can be?

7. What questions do you still have about embracing your differences?

Practice the Steps

Make a list of the steps you need to start practicing in your marriage this week.

1. Memorize Philippians 4:8.

2. As you begin to take note of how you and your spouse are different, commit that you will not allow the differences to become irritations, but instead will consider how those differences will become assets, making your marriage stronger.

3. Ask God to show you how your differences help you function better as a team. Commit to focusing on the positive.

4. _____

5. _____

Session 2

Do You Want to Dance?
and Connect the Partners

Chapter 3, pages 28-36 and Chapter 4, pages 37-55
from *The Marriage Dance*
For a better understanding of this topic, we suggest you read both chapters.

Chapter 3

Marriage encompasses a lifelong question: Are you and your partner willing to dance? Let's break the question into three parts. Answer the following questions about you—not your partner.

Do You Want to Dance?

Do *you* want to dance—or are you discouraged and bored with your marriage? Have you given up hope of a better marriage? Are you complacent? Have you decided your marriage is acceptable, and you don't need to meddle with something that ain't broke? If the decision were solely up to you, are *you* willing to dance?

Do you *want* to dance? It is impossible to force a person to dance. Your partner can push and shove—but that isn't dance. You can only invite a person to dance. What is your desire? If your partner invited you to dance, do you *want* to?

Do you want to *dance*? There are levels of desire. How strong is your desire? Maybe you're willing to stay in the relationship—but staying isn't dancing. If the household is running smoothly and fighting is minimal, that's still not "dancing." Do you want your relationship to dance? At what level do you want to dance? Are you willing to exert the effort to get it there?

God made us for relationship. Women seem to know this fact intuitively; most men agree after thinking about the idea for a short time. God's solution for man's need for relationship was to create woman (Genesis 2:18). Women emphasize maintaining a strong, loving family. Men often put more emphasis on providing for their family.

Commitment First

A close marriage relationship is built on emotional intimacy, commitment, and physical intimacy—in that order. These building blocks form a foundation of trust and commitment. When marriage is structured in this order, there is openness and vulnerability in each other's presence. Build trust and commitment first and then, sexual intimacy grows beyond expectations.

Reordering the priorities of marriage is not meant as a judgment of those who have built a relationship out of order. Putting physical intimacy first is common, accepted —even assumed in our society. We believe God set His order because He loves us. The foundation of trust must come first.

You may be saying, "Well, I would like to dance; my partner is the one who is refusing. What can I do?"

Consider what you might have done to dampen your partner's enthusiasm to dance. Start working to eliminate any block you created. Your partner may be blaming more on you than is realistic, but you need to eliminate any "real" blocks.

Invite your partner to dance with you. Offer as much relationship as he or she is willing to accept. Don't force; creatively invite.

When you invite, think of something enticing that your partner would like to do with you or that would be especially meaningful to them. For example, if they enjoy sporting events, suggest going to one together. If they like live theater, select a show that will facilitate conversation afterwards.

Learn to speak to your spouse's heart. If you believe your spouse has shut the relationship down or that your marriage is only running smoothly at the surface level, ask why. There may be problems underneath the surface that have been there a long time—possibly even before you married. Commit to working through those problems.

Pray for your spouse. Pray that God will expose any loneliness or pain. Let God reveal the reason his or her heart is locked up so tightly. Is his or her heart closed because of overt disobedience to God or shuttered to protect a still-open wound? What is he or she afraid of? Did you cause the wound? Pray for obedience, healing, and forgiveness according to what God shows you.

Have a serious discussion with no animosity, anger, or guilt trip. Say, "I need you." "I want you."

Even if these actions do not yield results, keep your heart open. Keep inviting and watching for opportunities. Persevere with respect and love. Develop a deep relationship with Jesus and allow Him to meet your emotional needs.

Fight for It

The picture God gives us of marriage in the Song of Solomon is one of physical attraction and delight, emotional intimacy, and sexual intimacy. But no relationship is perfect. Even in this seemingly exemplary relationship, there comes a period of apathy and separation (Song of Solomon 5). In the biblical story, the bride moves quickly to make amends. She puts herself in an uncomfortable and potentially dangerous situation to fight for the relationship. She could not predict if she would be able to find Solomon or if his heart would be open to her when she did. Nevertheless, she laid down her pride and took both the physical and emotional risk. Her marriage was worth it to her.

For those of you who are discouraged and don't believe your marriage can ever get better, we invite you to look at a photograph on *The Marriage Dance* website www. themarriagedance.com/2016/09/15/559/. Our son-in-law Nate captured the picture of this brilliant hot pink bouquet at Joshua Tree National Park. If you look closely, you'll see the flowers are growing out of the boulder—no soil, no water, nothing to fertilize them—but there they are. Nate entitled the photo *Impossible Isn't*.

If your marriage is struggling or boring, and you think it's impossible that it could get any better—it can. With God, "impossible—isn't."

Chapter 4

Connect the Partners

Connecting with your partner at a deep emotional level or "speaking to the heart" involves using the deepest part of you to care about the deepest part of your spouse. This kind of communication involves understanding that God gave us emotions, in part, to help us identify underlying pain. Painful emotions function the way physical pain does in our bodies, giving us important information about problem areas. Just as suppressing physical pain does not solve the problem in our body, neither does suppressing our emotions resolve our internal problems. Both physical and emotional pain tell you that you have a problem. To connect deeply with our spouse, we must both understand our emotions and seek to understand him or her.

Starting down the road to emotional intimacy, or connecting with your partner at a heart level, requires time and effort. The goal is to understand the forces that shaped your partner—not only at an intellectual level but at a heart level. Once you understand these forces, it will be easier to understand why your spouse reacts so strongly to what you say or do. Having a spouse who cares about you on this heart level brings healing to emotional pain.

Clear Communication

Connecting with your spouse involves communicating about more than family business and daily trivia. Conversations about daily life don't usually focus on understanding, cherishing, or respecting your spouse, nor do they draw you into emotional intimacy. But relating deeply allows your spouse to vent frustrations and gives your spouse the freedom to express emotions.

It may feel awkward to a man to be emotionally honest and vulnerable, but wives desire love and emotional connection and—although it may take men longer to realize it—men need emotional connection, too. These types of conversations are not always easy, but they are worth it. Connecting deeply with your partner takes communication from the head to the heart, and it binds your hearts together. Do not underestimate the power of open, loving communication and what it can accomplish in your marriage.

Heart's Desire

In marriage, there should be a desire to connect heart to heart. This connection means melding minds, hearts, thoughts, desires, motives, and goals and then, moving through life together as one flesh. The heart enables us to love, know God, laugh, feel passion, fight injustice, appreciate beauty—in short, to live. When the heart is wounded and dying, life withers and the glory of life fades.

A friend of ours wrote this poem to her husband. Could your spouse write something like this about you?

I Wanted You to Know Me

Osmosis does not make a marriage
I wanted us to cleave
My disappointment envelops
Too often, I want to leave.

Do you know my quirks;
Apprehension, fears?
Do you know
How often I shed tears?

Do you know me inside out,
Or outside in?
Do you know how often
I fantasize of sin?

To dream of one who wants me,
To know me to the core,
One who searches me
And still says, "more."

Do you know my wishes,
My, "someday I would like,"?
I want to dance in a purple dress
In the soft moonlight.

I am a romantic
Did you know?
Soft words, soft touches
Keep my flame aglow.

I want to read a million books
And strike the ivory keys
I want to paint pictures
And mediate mysteries.

I want to chat, throw out ideas
Contemplate anew
But you get angry
When thoughts don't fit your view.

I'm encased in a box
The funeral already happened.
I didn't know death had knocked.

Death. The death of a marriage.
The hope of soul mates gone.
You didn't want to know me.
I've been missing far too long.[1]

---

[1] Used by permission. Author wishes to remain anonymous.

Love requires action, but it needs more. Love demands compassion. Compassion motivates action. Both the Good Samaritan and the Prodigal's father had compassion that motivated them to action. When you compassionately care for and communicate with the heart of your spouse, you will find his or her deepest feelings unfolding. The emotional connection is a prerequisite for a long-term friendship at a heart level.

To develop an emotional connection with your spouse

- Set aside time—preferably every day—when you can give your full attention to your spouse. Allow half the time for each spouse to speak and be understood. This is not the time for chiming in, objecting, making suggestions or excuses or for blame. With practice, this safe time together will become natural and will flow into your normal conversations, too.

- Listen to your spouse. Listen not only to the words but also to the heart. Watch body language. Listen for needs, fears, concerns, loves, and joys.

- Understand the heart and emotions. What did his or her words mean? If necessary, say what you heard and ask if what you understood is correct. Beware of phrases that hold different meanings for a woman than they do for a man. For example, when a woman says, "I gained a couple of pounds last week," she may feel it is more significant than a man does. Share when you were embarrassed, filled with shame and bitterness as well as the happy and good moments. Probe, support, care for and pray about those areas. A caring spouse who hears and understands can eradicate years of lonely pain and create an intimate emotional bond.

- Celebrate special occasions, and celebrate for no reason at all. When you understand what makes your spouse feel alive and happy, you will be able to speak to them at a deep level.

- Communicate compassion. Pay attention to your mate's joys and wounds. Don't be too quick. Stay with a subject until your spouse knows they have been heard and understood.

Conversation Starters

Talk about childhood experiences—incidents and encounters that positively and negatively influenced your spouse's early years. Conversation is not about solving the problem. Instead, the conversation is to show that you care about the heartache.

"Rejoice with those who rejoice and weep with those who weep" (Romans 12:15).

You can find a list of emotional intimacy questions on pages 47-51 and Appendices B, C, and D of *The Marriage Dance* (pages 176-187).

Talk about the joys and challenges of your marriage. Stay with the safe questions until you have covered Chapters 7-10. If your spouse tells you they often feel alone, ask a follow-up question. "Will you give me an example?" Listen and understand. You might say something to show you understand, "That must have been very painful." If you feel safe, ask these questions, "Do I make you feel alone?" "How do I do that?" Don't defend yourself. Listen. Then say, "I'm sorry. I don't ever want to make you feel that way." (Remember compassion first and then, action.)

Deeper Conversations

The goal of conversation is to go beyond the surface to build a connection that will eliminate the need for disagreements or fights. "I want you to know that I care that you feel that way and if I did something to fracture our relationship, I'm sorry." Deeper conversations make both spouse's hearts come alive. Here are some tips for starting deeper conversations.

- Ask your spouse how his or her heart is. Try asking how the "little girl" or "little boy" is doing today and how you can love that little girl or little boy.

- Tell your spouse you want to do anything to help them be free inside.

- Say that you want to make a safe place for your spouse to share.

Beware of Two Common Mis-steps

1. Don't try to solve the problem. Don't inject your "superior" problem-solving skills unless your spouse asks for help.

2. Don't try to protect yourself from what your spouse says. Defending yourself will stymie important two-way communication. Self-protective communication is even more difficult when both spouses are defending themselves at the same time. Listen to your spouse's perspective. Is there something the team should do differently?

This way of communicating may seem hard at first, but openness, honesty, and genuineness will go a long way toward connecting.

Improve Your Technique

Chapter 3

If you have time, read Song of Solomon—preferably in a newer translation.

Rewrite Song of Solomon 1:15-16a using your words as though you were saying them to your spouse. Feel free to change the gender as necessary and remember to compliment a characteristic you genuinely admire about your spouse even if it is not mentioned in the original text.

Read Mark 10:1-12. (Jesus quotes Genesis 2:24.) What does Jesus say about divorce? (Bonus: Cross-reference this passage with Matthew 19:3-12.)

Do you believe you were made for relationship? Why do you think so?

Do *you* want to dance? If it were completely up to you, are you committed to your marriage?

Do you *want to* dance? Is your heart in your marriage? Do you want a deep relationship or are you performing out of duty because you think God wants you to?

Do you want to *dance*? Do you want a marriage that delights your heart? Are you willing to do what it takes to get that deep connection? At what level do you want to dance?

Does an intimate emotional relationship seem like a big risk to you? What are you afraid of?

Do you think your spouse is willing to dance? Do you believe your spouse wants an intimate emotional relationship? Why or why not? In what areas? Ask God what you can do to help your spouse want that deeper level of connection.

Do you think you and your spouse have the same expectations for your marriage? If not, how do they differ? Why do they differ?

What examples from your marriage would be a good example for other couples?

What examples merely show that you are satisfied with your marriage?

What examples show that your marriage needs work?

Chapter 4

Look up the following verses. Re-write each one using your words.

Proverbs 12:18

Proverbs 4:23

Proverbs 15:4

Proverbs 15:23

Proverbs 18:21

1 Thessalonians 5:11

1 Peter 3:9

As a whole, what do these verses tell you about the power of the tongue? Do the principles apply to both positive words and negative words?

What are some examples of how the principles of the tongue would apply when talking to your spouse?

Would you say communication with your spouse is open and easy or are there certain areas that always provoke an uneasy response and which need to be tip-toed around?

What are the problem areas?

1. _____

2. _____

3. _____

Who gets irritated—you or your spouse—and on which areas?

1. _____

2. _____

3. _____

Do you know why those areas cause problems? Ask God to give insight to you, and then write your responses.

How do the verses you looked up at the beginning of this section apply to those troublesome areas?

Would you like it if you and your spouse could regularly speak to each other in a way that made you feel cherished, respected, accepted, safe, confident, adequate, and wise?

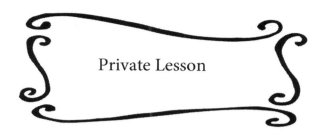

Private Lesson

Chapter 3

Ask God to direct your discussion to the areas and issues you need to discuss.

Compare the answers you wrote about your expectations with your spouse's responses. How do they differ? Why do they differ? What do your answers say about God in your marriage?

Tell your spouse about a time when you felt emotionally connected to him or her. Explain how he or she helped create that connection. Discuss how to build these kinds of emotional encounters into your marriage on a regular basis?

Bonus: Read through the Song of Solomon together.

Is Song of Solomon a picture of what a marriage relationship can be like? If not, what is its purpose in the Bible? (Consider the following verses: Song of Solomon 1:2; 2:16; 4:10; 5:4-6; 7:10-12.

Do you think a relationship like the one modeled by Solomon and the Shulamite woman is possible? Why or why not?

Share your re-write of Song of Solomon 1:15-16a with your spouse.

Ask God to help you resolve any problem areas.

Chapter 4

Ask God to direct your discussion to the areas and issues you need to discuss.

- Allow a minimum of 20 minutes for this exercise.
- Choose a time when you are not likely to be interrupted.
- Sit in a comfortable place where you can look at each other—knee-to-knee.
- Hold hands.
- Select a question from the list below.
- One spouse should share first while the other spouse listens and does not interrupt or defend.
- Then the other spouse speaks.
- As you listen, hear not only the words but listen for any emotions to surface.

- Ask clarifying questions to draw your spouse out more.
- This is not a speed drill.
- The goal is not to make it through all the questions.
- The goal is to understand your spouse better than you have before and to "speak words of life" to them.
- Ask God to help you.
- If you pick one question and give each spouse a chance to speak, you have completed the assignment.
- If you would like to go further, you may. Or, you may take another question at another time.
- Try to go deep on the question.
- Explore its depths.
- Follow-up on the initial answer with questions such as, "Tell me more." "How did that affect you?" "How does it affect you today?"

1. What have you enjoyed most about the years we've been together?

2. Describe one of the happiest periods in our relationship.

3. When we're together, what do you enjoy doing most?

4. What's going on inside right now?

5. Are you ever afraid? Of what?

6. What causes you to be discouraged?

7. How can I communicate my love for you? Please suggest gifts or actions.

Ask God to help you resolve any problem areas.

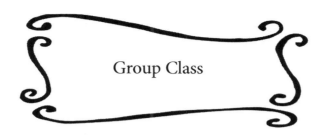

Group Class

Chapter 3

1. What would you recommend to someone who is tired of marriage because his or her partner has given up on the idea of a relationship?

2. What character traits, attitudes, and commitments help create emotional connection?

3. Bonus: For those who read Song of Solomon, do you think a relationship like the one modeled by Solomon and the Shulamite woman is possible? Why or why not? Do you think their relationship will change over time? Is this change good or bad?

Chapter 4

1. In what ways is "life and death in the power of the tongue" in marriage?

2. What impressed you about the "Speak to the Heart" exercise?

3. What benefits do you see in taking the time to speak to each other this way?

4. What obstacles did you run into?

5. What questions do you have?

6. What can you share that your spouse said would be a meaningful gift you could give? Why is that gift so meaningful?

7. Did your spouse say something to you that encouraged you and gave you a new perspective that you could share with the group?

8. Can you see value in speaking to each other's heart over time? How would this help or encourage you?

Practice the Steps

Chapter 3 & 4

1. Ask God how you can best connect with your spouse's heart.

2. Brainstorm with your spouse activities the two of you like to do together.

3. Have a three-way conversation with your spouse and God to discuss the depth of your marriage and the potential for improving it.

4. Set aside at least 20 minutes, follow the guidelines and practice speaking to each other's heart.

5. _____

Session 3

Lead with Confidence

Chapter 5, pages 56-70 from *The Marriage Dance*
For a better understanding of this topic, we suggest you read the full chapter.

God has ordained authority. There are countless examples of people who used authority well. Unfortunately, there are also numerous examples of people who used their authority poorly. The problem is not leadership; the problem is bad leadership. The solution is not to eliminate leadership. The solution is to learn good leadership.

Why Men Sometimes Don't Lead
- Sometimes men don't know what to do.
- Sometimes, as in dance, marriage is complicated. There is much to know and do.
- Sometimes a man has to struggle with his wife over who will lead.
- Sometimes a man may feel inadequate to lead.
- Sometimes a man may fear being criticized.
- Sometimes our culture encourages men to step aside and let women take over the leadership roles. The decision spills over into marriage as well.
- Sometimes the balance between leading and forcing is hard to find and maintain.

How Jesus Led

Good leadership requires service. In our culture, leadership is often associated with power. However, Jesus gave up His glory as God, became a man, and lived as an unknown for 30 years. He washed his disciples' feet and, the next day, allowed Himself to be tortured and to die on a Roman cross. Who else would define leadership by this example? This is the kind of leadership husbands are asked to exhibit in Ephesians 5:25, "Husbands love your wives just as Christ also loved the Church and gave Himself up for her." Jesus said anyone who wanted to be great must be the servant of all. (Matthew 25:25-28; Mark 10:42-45; Luke 22:25-27; and John 13:13-15.) This kind of leadership is beautiful and inspiring—not arrogant and heavy-handed.

Essential Leadership

In dance, leading is not controversial; it is essential. If two different people are going to dance together in close proximity without stepping on each other, someone has to decide which steps to do and make it happen. Assuming a man is willing to lead, he can learn about leadership from dance. God gave husbands the leadership role.

Are You Willing to Lead?

Commit to lead. A maxim in dance says, "The man is the structure; the woman is the beauty," or "The man is the frame; the woman is the picture." The man provides the structure of the dance by leading the steps, but the woman is showcased as she turns, twirls, kicks, and provides the beauty. The roles are different but equal in importance. Men must step into the leadership role and lead.

If a man wants to ensure his partner will have a good time, he will protect her from colliding with other dancers as they move around the floor, and make it fun and comfortable for his partner to dance. A man who leads well focuses on how well he can get his partner to dance. If she dances beautifully and is having a good time, he has led well. Leading well requires him to serve his partner. Women love to dance with a man who leads well. Service and sacrifice also define leadership in a Christian marriage.

Lead with your core—your torso—your center. When a man leads from his core, his partner immediately feels it and can respond. The principle works the same way in marriage. If a man leads from the core of his being—from a consistent character of integrity, his wife knows what to expect and how to respond. See Boaz's example in Ruth 3:18.

Communicate clearly with your partner or she will be unable to respond and contribute to the plan. If you are truly on the same team, your wife's insights, opinions, and perspectives are good news—not bad news. A wise husband realizes his wife is helping him avoid problems and failures. Listening to your teammate is good leadership. If you listen, you improve your chances of success.

Have a plan. In dances that move around the floor, such as Waltz, Foxtrot, and Tango, the leader has to know which steps will keep him facing the line of dance, which steps will turn him on a diagonal, and which steps will take him around a corner. He also has to estimate how much room the step will take and determine if the couple can do it in the space available. In other words, he has to know what to do and have a plan. Likewise, a strong leader in marriage must have a plan. A husband will find his wife a more willing follower if she knows he has a good plan.

Look out for your partner's welfare even in unexpected circumstances. On the dance floor and in marriage, there are surprises. A good leader is alert and protects his partner from them.

Be gentle. "Strong but gentle" is not an oxymoron. Leaders who whip their partners around and hurt them soon have no partners to dance with. In marriage, strong but gentle might sound like, "I think this is the direction we should go, but please pray about it and tell me what you think."

Keep learning. There is much to learn both in dance and in marriage. In marriage and life, the Bible is the syllabus that teaches you what you should do. Study and keep learning.

Fulfill your responsibility. In dance, both partners are responsible for staying in time with the music, maintaining a strong dance frame, and doing the step correctly. In marriage, both partners are responsible for maintaining a strong relationship with God as well as taking care of the things your partner cannot or should not do.

In dance, the man chooses the step. He sets the direction. But a good leader uses his partner's strengths to benefit the team. In marriage, a wise husband uses his spouse's expertise, talents, background, and gifts for the benefit of the team.

Learn from your mistakes. The question is not whether you'll make mistakes but whether you'll learn from them. Mistakes give you valuable feedback. Don't be afraid of them. After you make a mistake, pause and learn from it.

Give time to adjust. In dance, it's not fair to make a sudden move without giving your partner time to adjust and respond. In marriage, your wife needs time to respond. The bigger the change (e.g. a major move, a career change), the more "lead time" you need to give. Answer her doubts and make sure she doesn't have any concerns you haven't thought of or planned for.

Realize the leader may need to adjust. The leader can lead, but if the partner can't take as large of a step, the leader must adjust. This is an essential part of being a wise and courteous leader.

Be persistent. Have a strong will to glorify God. The better you want to dance, the more you need to persevere. In marriage, both the consequences and rewards are greater than in dance.

Be righteous. Keep your actions pure. Live with nothing to hide.

Do you doubt that your wife wants you to lead? Ask her, "If I led in our marriage the way leading is described in this chapter, would you like it?" See what she says. Don't be afraid of struggling to lead. Your wife will almost certainly be patient and supportive if she knows you are trying to lead well.

Commitment is the Key

The first step in learning to lead well is committing to the journey. This is not a feature of the intellect or the emotions. It is a decision of the will. Make the decision to have a good marriage and then courageously take the actions necessary to have one.

Second, consider asking a marriage mentor to help you focus on what you can improve to get to the next level in marriage. After all, if you didn't know a dance step, would you hesitate to ask a dance instructor or a more competent dancer for help?

It may take longer than you wish to become a good leader, but it is beautiful for two people to move together as one.

Improve Your Technique

Read John 13:5-12. Jesus led with service and sacrifice. What would this look like in a 21ˢᵗ-century marriage? Give specific examples of how you "wash your spouse's feet."

In your marriage, what would it mean for the husband to "lead from his core"? Be specific.

Questions for Husbands

Read Ephesians 5:25-33. Describe what it would mean to lead like this in your marriage.

Read Philippians 2:3-8. Ask God to reveal whether or not you lead in such a way that gives value to your wife's interests. Ask Him to expose areas in which you lead from selfish motives. Listen for His answers and write them in the space below.

Do you feel comfortable leading? When do you *not* feel comfortable leading? What prevents you from leading? What would you need to learn to feel comfortable?

Read God's charge to Joshua, the new leader of the Israelites, as he was about to lead the people into the Promised Land (Joshua 1:6-9). What words stand out to you? In what areas of your life do you need to implement this command?

Read 1 Corinthians 16:13 and I Kings 2:2. What does it mean to act like a man? Bonus question: Have you ever sabotaged your leadership? How?

If learning to lead well takes longer than you thought it would, are you willing to persevere?

Questions for Wives

If your husband were a strong but gentle leader as described in this chapter, would you enjoy his leadership? Are you willing to be patient and supportive while he learns? What might patience cost you?

Ask God to show you if you sometimes resist your husband's leadership. How do you do it? Why do you resist?

What do you see as the biggest impediment to your husband being a good leader? How do you think that impediment can be removed?

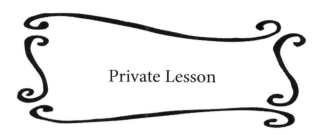

Private Lesson

Ask God to direct your discussion to the areas and issues you need to discuss.

Husbands, share with your wife whether you feel she wants you to lead. Why have you come to that conclusion?

Wives, if your husband led in a strong but gentle way in your home, would you welcome that or not? Tell your husband about your feelings.

What are some of the areas in your marriage where there is friction over leadership?

Bonus question: Husbands, ask your wife for an assessment of your leadership style. Wives, what do you think are your husband's strengths in the area of leading? His weaknesses? Talk about the areas in which—by agreement—your wife should take the initiative or primary responsibility.

Ask God to help you resolve any problem areas.

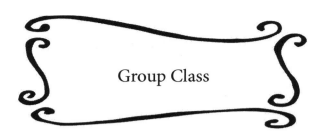

Group Class

1. What questions do you have from your Improve Your Technique or Private Lesson?

2. Share your thoughts about whether you believe God wants men to lead the family.

3. What does our society say about leadership? Which of those messages do you believe are true? Which of those messages do you believe are false?

4. What are some of the obstacles in our society that make it difficult for men to lead?

5. What would servant-leadership look like in 21st century marriages? (See Matthew 20:25-28; Mark 10:42-45; Luke 22:25-27; and John 13:13-15.)

6. What are the practical steps that would help a man to "lead from his core" in marriage?

7. Bonus question: What are some lessons you have learned from leading in the past?

8. Bonus question: When you have a question about your marriage, where do you go to get answers?

Practice the Steps

1. Decide on a mentor couple you both feel comfortable asking for advice.

2. _____

3. _____

4. _____

Session 4

Follow with Strength

Chapter 6, pages 71-88 from *The Marriage Dance*
For a better understanding of this topic, we suggest you read the full chapter.

A good follower is strong, knowledgeable, and proficient. A dancer who is not strong enough to hold her arms up for the duration of a dance begins to lean on her partner and drag both of them down. She needs to know the steps and what is expected of her. She uses her unique style to add beauty, fun, and creativity to the dance. In ballroom dance, even though the woman follows the man, she is the one who gets showcased.

A Follower is Strong
In the same way, a proficient "helper" (Genesis 2:18) or "follower" must be a strong person who knows what she is doing. She seeks God's direction for her family and brings those thoughts and ideas into discussions with her husband. She uses all the tools God has given her to benefit her family. And, hopefully, she adds fun, spice, and excitement as well.

Equally Different
We support the biblical concept that God created two, equal joint heirs. We believe a wife should give her husband final authority and acknowledge him as the head and leader of the family. If there is still a sincere disagreement after the subject has been discussed and opinions, insights, and perspectives have been shared, we recommend the following:
A wife should tell her husband.

I intend to support your decision. (She should only say it if she means it.)

I see the following problem(s), or I have the following concerns. Be specific and non-condemning.

In the past, we've run into the following obstacles when trying something like this. Remain specific and neutral. (Don't say, "Remember the last time you made a mistake!")

Then, pray together.

This kind of conversation is helpful to the marriage.

- It encourages the wife to use the gifts and insights God has given her.

- It communicates that husband and wife are on the same team.

- It eliminates the perception of a personal attack and spotlights specific honest concerns. It takes the fight out of the discussion.

- In taking this approach, a wife positions her husband to pray, ponder, and make a wise decision (also called "leading"). The buck now stops with him. The husband will also know that if it is the wrong decision, it will be his responsibility.

- If a husband refuses advice and does not seek God, God will correct him on His timetable and in His way.

Some wives will ask the husband to lead, but if he leads in a direction she doesn't like, that same wife will succumb to the temptation to take the lead from him. Wives must understand that a refusal to release control encourages husbands to stop leading. Understandably, this refusal makes husbands angry, and the wife's control becomes a message that the husband is not needed or is incompetent. Whether he says it aloud or silently, his response is, "Fine, if you want to lead, you go right ahead." A better approach is for wives to communicate how much the husband is needed, and appreciated.

Wives might consider some self-analysis and these questions.

- Have you damaged your husband's heart?

- Have you made it difficult for your husband to lead?"

- Do you listen to your husband's answer without defending yourself?

- Have you asked him for forgiveness?

- Have other people in his life said or done things which make it hard for him to lead?"

- Have you told him about the good qualities you see in him?

- Have you invited him to lead?

A wife cannot have it both ways. She cannot take over the lead and then complain when her husband doesn't want to lead.

Stay in the Arm

In dance, following involves more than performing the steps the man indicates. It also involves staying in the man's arm. When a woman "stays in the arm," she matches the timing, size, and style of his steps. If the lady tries to make the man do the dance her way, they will be at odds with each other rather than function as a team. In marriage, if a wife sets her heart to be sensitive and responsive, to match her man step-for-step and movement-for-movement, they will move together as one.

Genesis 2:18 says, "Then the Lord God said, 'It is not good for the man to be alone; I will make him a helper suitable for him.'" When you say it in English, the word "helper" can sound demeaning. In Hebrew, the term is *ezer*. As Stasi Eldredge explains in her book *Captivating*, ezer is never used in the Old Testament to describe a subordinate. Rather, the word is used to describe God as our helper. (See Exodus 18:4; Deuteronomy 33:26, 29; Psalm 33:20; 70:5; 115:9;10,11; 121:1-2; 124:8; and 146:5.). Moses named his younger son Eliezer—"God is my helper." (Eli – my God; ezer – helper)

Tone and Resistance

Another principle couples must master to dance is called tone and resistance. As they join hands and hold each other in the dance frame, they exert a gentle but constant and cooperative tension on each other. This position accomplishes several results. First, it prevents them from stepping on each other. Second, as long as the gentle resistance is maintained, when the man steps forward or sideways or into a turn, the lady can feel it and respond. If the lady does not maintain her tone and resistance but rather, collapses like a wet noodle, it is difficult for the man to lead. Her gentle resistance helps him to lead better.

Following does not preclude the wife from participating in the decisions. On the contrary, partners who work well together bring individual gifts, insights, and life experiences to the decision-making table. The cooperative tension between them enables them to make a better decision. Make special note of the word "cooperative." In no way is the tension a hostile shoving match. Rather, two people are working together to achieve a superior result.

Trust

It is the man's responsibility to keep the couple safe on the dance floor. If the lady does not trust him and looks backward over her shoulder to survey the situation herself, she will throw the couple off balance. In some of the dance "stunts" like the death drop in which the man catches his partner by the neck just before she hits the floor, trust is essential. One competitive dancer told us that it was when she didn't trust her partner and tried to second guess him that she got hurt. Of course, her male partner had to demonstrate trustworthiness. Family situations also require trust. It takes time plus consistent action to develop deep trust.

Sometimes the Wife Leads

Some ballroom steps require the woman to lead (or "go first") for part of the step. The Twinkle and Weave in Waltz, for example, requires the man to send the lady in front of him causing her body weight to pull him through into the next part of the step. Something similar happens in marriage when the wife takes the lead in specific areas— perhaps because they agree the wife has superior talents in those areas. The key is that she takes the lead by agreement; she does not grab the lead. There is a huge difference between, "I accept the lead in a certain area because that is what's best for the team," and, "I'm taking the lead because you are incompetent."

Challenging

In both dance and marriage, a wife encourages a more difficult but more beautiful step by being strong enough to do it herself. She is then able to challenge her partner to match her. For example, in marriage, if she starts memorizing Scripture, steps up her exercise routine, or chooses to read one educational book a month, she may challenge her husband to make positive changes in those areas as well.

Blind Spots

Neither the man nor the woman can see behind them on the dance floor. In those cases, it is the partner's responsibility to warn of danger. In Quickstep, the speed of the dance increases the importance of the woman's warning of danger in the blind spot. Wise partners will heed a spouse's warning immediately. If not, there could be a nasty pile-up. In marriage, both partners should be alert for potential blind spots and communicate the danger. Any wise partner should be thankful for the insight to avoid the problem he couldn't see. Taking the initiative in this area goes both ways.

Misconceptions about Following

In our culture, following or submission is often viewed as a position of inferiority. The dictionary defines submission as "giving in to the power, authority, or desires of another." However, when we look at Jesus' example, he submitted His will to the Father's—not because He was forced, but as a gift of love. Philippians 2:5-11 tells us Jesus submitted His will to the Father and as a result was highly exalted by the Father. In dance, the woman follows, but she is the one who is showcased. Using the biblical description, the command for a wife to submit to her husband as to the Lord in Ephesians 5:22, 24 should not be taken as a woman acquiescing to an inferior position. Rather, it is a gift that a wife chooses to give. In any multi-person team, someone needs to take leadership so the team can function. The person making the decisions is not superior. Leadership is merely a function that must be undertaken for the team to function well.

Suppose He Makes A Mistake

Wives, what does your marriage dance look like when you think your husband is wrong? Do you dig in your heels? Do you try to take over? Are you up front and loud about your refusal or do you just make sure his idea never gets to the top of the "to do" list? Husbands, what does your marriage dance look like when you refuse to listen to your wife's suggestions or ideas? Do you dig in your heels? Do you force your leadership? Do you push your idea to the top of the agenda?

Instead of subverting the plan, why not discuss your concerns and frustrations openly. Ask your spouse to pray about the matter. Then put the matter in God's hands.

Both husbands and wives make mistakes. Practice giving your partner the same grace you would like to receive when it's your turn to be wrong. Instead of ridicule, try these words:

"I know you made a mistake, but I love you madly anyway."

"It's not the end of the world. It's not even close."

Twice, Abraham's lies about Sarah being his sister landed her in the harem of a pagan king. (Genesis 12 and Genesis 20) Most wives would be understandably furious if their husband did that, but 1 Peter 3:5-6 says that Sarah submitted to him and called him her master. How could she do this? We believe it is because she put her ultimate trust in God—and God performed two miracles to protect her despite Abraham's failures.

In beginning dance, the men often made mistakes in leading the steps. They were just learning. The ladies had a choice: They could tell them they made a mistake and refuse to go on, or they could follow. From our observations, the men usually self-corrected within a few measures, and they learned from their mistakes much faster than when their partner corrected them.

In marriage, husbands, too, will make mistakes as they learn to lead. We think they will learn faster if their wives are willing to encourage them and keep following even though they share the danger of the mistake.

Improve Your Technique

Questions for both Husbands and Wives

Read the following verses.

> "An excellent wife, who can find? For her worth is far above jewels. The heart of her husband trusts in her, and he will have no lack of gain. She does him good and not evil all the days of her life. . . Her children rise up and bless her; her husband also, and he praises her saying: 'Many daughters have done nobly, but you excel them all.' Charm is deceitful, and beauty is vain, but a woman who fears the Lord, she shall be praised." Proverbs 31:10-12 and 28-30

List 3-5 adjectives that describe this woman.

Is this picture of the Proverbs 31 wife consistent with the descriptions you have heard of the "submissive wife" in the past? What new insights did you get from this passage? What misconceptions did you have?

Ezer (helper) is used in the following passages: Psalm 10:14; 30:10; 54:4; 70:5; 72:12; 121:2. Look up the verses and see what new understanding of "helper" these verses give you?

Questions for Wives

Do you trust your husband to make hard decisions? If you don't, why not? Are you willing to trust God and pray for your husband?

What might be some advantages of giving your husband final authority?

Do you believe God would teach your husband to lead well if you stepped back and let Him?

Ask God if you have damaged your husband's heart and his willingness to lead by grabbing the lead yourself. If God brings any areas or incidents to mind, write them here.

What do you do in your life that challenges your husband to grow in his life?

Write a prayer for your husband to become a godly servant-leader.

Questions for Husbands

Does your wife follow your lead? How? (If so, be sure to compliment her on it.)

How can you help your wife be a better follower?

Write a prayer for your wife to become a "God-like" helper.

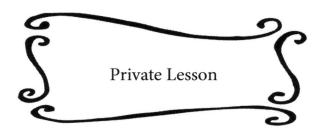

Private Lesson

Ask God to direct your discussion to the areas and issues you need to discuss.

Wives, ask your husband if other people said or did things in the past that make it hard for him to lead now. Did anything about his past life experience affect his ability to lead? Ask him if you do the same type of thing. (Listen and don't defend yourself.)

Wives, ask your husband if you have done things that have made it hard for him to lead. Ask him if you have a tendency to "take over." In what areas do you take over? How do you do it? (Listen to him and don't defend yourself.) If he says you have, consider asking his forgiveness. If you can say it from the heart, tell your husband you would welcome his lead.

In your marriage, in what areas do you agree, as a couple, that the wife should take the initiative and primary responsibility?

Discuss what leading and following should look like in your marriage. What adjustments do you need to make? How would your marriage be different if the "follower" were more willing to let go of the reins?

Ask God to help you resolve any problem areas.

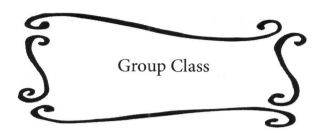

Group Class

1. In dance, "staying in the arm" means the lady must match the man's pace, size of steps, and style. As a practical matter, what do you think this looks like in marriage?

2. How does a wife give her husband tone and resistance in marriage? Give some practical examples.

3. What examples do you know of where a wife tried to warn her husband of a blind spot? Did he listen or not? What was the result? Do you have any examples where a husband warned his wife?

4. Did anyone try praying for their spouse rather than nagging them? What was the result?

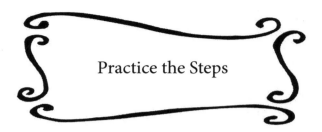

Practice the Steps

What steps should you take this week to start implementing these principles?

1. Next time you disagree with your husband, pray for him rather than taking control.

2. _____

3. _____

Session 5

Sin: Bitterness

Chapter 7A, pages 89-97 in *The Marriage Dance*
For a better understanding of this topic, we suggest you read the full chapter.

Because sin is such an important area, we will spend three weeks on chapter 7. The next two sessions will also deal with Chapter 7.

Introduction

Two ballroom dancers stand in the middle of the floor. There is a serious problem with the man. Instead of holding his partner in dance position, he is standing in a defensive position characteristic of martial artists. His partner is trying to get close enough to hold him—to dance with him—but she can't. He turns warily, shielding himself behind his raised arm. If she reaches in towards him, he responds with a chop, jab, or kick. Dancing with a partner in battle stance is impossible. The result would be the same if the lady took a defensive position.

Both men and women bring defenses and other baggage into marriage. We develop coping mechanisms in response to life situations. We control, or we hide. Life has taught us we must protect ourselves. Self-protection creates relational tension. We keep others, including our mate, at arm's length and beyond. Marriage does not cause the problems; it merely reveals the problems that we brought into the marriage.

Go Back

In dance, proper form on one step leads to proper form on the next step. But if a step went wrong in the past, it can cause a misstep in the future. You have to go back and get it right.

You may have noticed in your marriage that some problems keep repeating themselves or that your reaction or your spouse's is out of proportion to the problem. The same principle that is true in dance is also true in your marriage. If there is something wrong from the past, it will continue causing problems until it gets straightened out and you learn to do it right.

While any sin negatively affects your life and your marriage, in the next three sessions we will be focusing on six common "missteps" that destroy spiritual strength as well as marital harmony. The key to success is to focus on your issues, not your spouse's.

Bitterness

Bitterness goes beyond mere anger. It is resentment towards someone who has hurt you. You may have a desire for revenge. You may have put up a wall of self-protection so you cannot be reached. You may hate the person. It is not your fault that another person wronged or hurt you, but if you allow yourself to become bitter, it is your responsibility.

Ephesians 4:31 commands us to put away bitterness and resentment. Hebrews 12:15 says, "See to it that no one comes short of the grace of God; that no root of bitterness springing up causes trouble and by it many be defiled" (NASB). Romans 12:19 says, "Never take your revenge, beloved, but leave room for the wrath of God, for it is written, 'Vengeance is mine, I will repay,' says the Lord."

One problem with bitterness is that the resentment you feel toward one person gets taken out on someone else when the emotional situation is similar. For example, a wife explodes at her husband when he does something that reminds her of the father with whom she is still angry.

The Solution

The solution for bitterness is forgiving the real offender. Jesus' teaching on bitterness is a story recorded in Matthew 18:21 – 35. Take a moment and read that story now. As long as you harbor bitterness, you cannot reach freedom in your marriage even if the bitterness was not originally toward your spouse.

The problem of bitterness is central to God's gospel message. God is willing to forgive our enormous debt. Consider God's perspective. God sent his perfect son to die in our place for our rebellion against Him, and we are unwilling to forgive someone who hurt us. God went to great expense to forgive us, and we are not willing to forgive others who have hurt us.

Forgiveness does not mean ignoring the pain or justifying wrongdoing. God asks us to forgive because we have been forgiven. Forgiving releases the torment caused by the bitterness. It is still up to God to provide justice in the long term or to take vengeance (Romans 12:19).

Forgive

Forgive the person and release the bitterness and resentment toward the one who sinned against you. As you do, God may show you why that person acted the way they did. They may have acted out of hurt and pain. Perhaps they default to a pattern modeled to them. God may give you compassion and understanding towards them even though the act itself was wrong. The things we hold in bitterness are given an honored place in our memory. We cannot truly thank God for his incomparable forgiveness if we hang on to others' offenses in our past. We cannot freely relate to those around us – especially our spouse – while the root of bitterness is doing its insidious work inside us.

Releasing the Bitterness

To release bitterness, admit that holding a grudge is wrong. Choose to forgive the person who hurt you. Stop allowing the consequences of bitterness to control your life. Pray a simple prayer like this one: "Lord, [person's name] hurt me badly and caused me a lot of pain. Instead of forgiving them like you want me to do, I have been hanging onto a grudge for a long time. That grudge has made me bitter. Now my heart is cold and hard toward them. Bitterness has also hurt my relationships with those around me. It's hard for me to let go, but now, I choose to obey and forgive. I choose to forgive despite the wrong act. I let [name of person] off my hook. I am willing to bear the consequences I suffered and forgive. Amen."

Some people do not understand how to pray. It is simple. Just talk to God. You don't have to speak out loud, but you can if you want. Pause and give Him a chance to answer you. He might answer by putting a thought in your mind or by giving you a mental image or by bringing to mind something you've heard in the past. His answers will never conflict with the Bible. He doesn't always answer immediately. You may need to pray for a month or even longer. Wait and watch for His answer. Practice praying and get good at it. Learn to hear God's inaudible voice.

If God brought a particular person or grievance to your mind as you've been reading this section, start with that person or situation.

Forgive it All

Forgive all the grievances that are still bothering you. If someone continues to bother you, there is a blockage in your relationship. Ask God to show you the specific cause of the break in the relationship. Make a list. Then, pray through the list. Look at the problem from the other person's perspective. Did you cause part of the problem? Were they hurt by others and they were perpetuating what had been done to them? What can you do to break the cycle? Continue to ask for God's help until you have forgiven the offense from your heart. You will know you have truly forgiven when you feel an inner freedom and when the internal turmoil becomes calm. When you have truly forgiven, you will find the anger and frustration are gone, and the disharmony in your other relationships calms down as well.

Pray that God will help you emotionally understand the exorbitant price God paid to forgive you. When we understand the depth of our transgression, it is easier to forgive those who injured us. If you feel you can't forgive, ask God for His help to be *willing* to forgive. Let Him help. Be patient; some bitterness is so deep it takes time.

Consider the people you may need to forgive: Someone who came to mind as you read this, a spouse who treated you without love or respect, a parent who did not parent well, a sibling who treated you in a high-handed way, a boss who gave you the terrible assignment no one else wanted, a teacher who ridiculed you in class, a bully. Ask God to reveal bitterness in your heart.

Forgive Yourself

Are you mad at yourself for doing something stupid or for not being up to the task at hand? Don't forget to forgive yourself. Ask God if you need to forgive yourself. If he says "yes," go through the process.

Forgive God

Is there any situation that makes you feel mad at God? A heartless family? A physical deformity or ailment? God allowed you to be the victim of an attack? Ask God to spotlight any bitterness you may be harboring toward Him. If God brings something to your mind, ask God to help you resolve and remove it. Tell God you are sorry for not believing that He causes all things to work together for good (Romans 8:28) and release Him from the grudge you've been holding against Him. God doesn't need to be forgiven, but going through the forgiveness process may help you. Ask God for a stronger faith that He is working in you through this situation.

Improve Your Technique

Read the following passages. What does each one direct you to do?

Matthew 18:21-35

Ephesians 4:3

Hebrews 12:15

Romans 12:19

Ask God if you are harboring bitterness toward anybody. In the space below, write the names that come to mind.

Is bitterness affecting your marriage and other relationships? How?

Use the worksheet to work through bitterness. Be thorough. Bitterness is a sin God cares deeply about. If you are not willing to forgive others, why should God forgive you? Harboring bitterness will affect your spiritual, emotional, and physical health.

It will affect your interpersonal relationships, your ability to love and be loved, your marriage, your children, your attitude toward other people, and life itself. Experience the freedom that God wants you to experience.

Don't skim through this assignment.

WORKSHEET: BITTERNESS - PEOPLE WHO HAVE HURT ME

Adapted from Biblical Concepts Counseling, John Regier, used by permission

Consider parents, siblings, spouse, others. Do you think God has hurt you? Are there areas where you can't forgive yourself?

List people who have hurt you	Answer the question, "What am I feeling?" Describe the emotional pain (See Emotional Pain Words page 77-78)	How did they hurt you?	Identify your response?

Suggested Prayer:

"Lord, _____[person's name]_____ hurt me badly. Instead
of forgiving them like you want me to do, I have been hanging onto
a grudge for a long time. That grudge has made me bitter. Now my
heart is cold and hard. Bitterness also hurts my relationships with those
around me. It's hard for me to let go, but I choose to obey and forgive.
What he/she did caused me great pain, but I choose to forgive despite
that wrong act. I let [name of person] off the hook. I am willing to
bear the consequences I suffered and forgive. Amen."

Invite Jesus to Comfort Your Painful Memories

This exercise involves prayer—asking God some questions, listening intently and
waiting patiently. You were hurt and developed bitterness because someone caused you
physical, emotional, or spiritual pain. Ask God to heal the pain as well as the bitterness.

For each painful memory you listed in the first worksheet, ask God these questions.

1. "Lord, were You there when [painful memory] happened?" Listen. Wait for a
    response.

2. "Where were You?"

3. "Lord, what would You do if I gave this pain to You? Please heal my pain."

Emotional Pain Words

Chart: *Biblical Concepts in Counseling*, John Regier, used by permission
Use this chart to aid you in identifying the type of pain you experienced.

Abandoned	Foolish	Publicly shamed
Accused	Forced	Rejected
Afraid	Frustrated	Rejection
All my fault	Good for nothing	Repulsed
Alone	Guilty	Revenge
Always wrong	Hated	Ruined
Angry	Hate myself	Sad
Anxious	Helpless	Scared
Apathetic	Hollow	Secluded
Ashamed	Hopeless	Self-disgust
Bad	Humiliated	Shamed
Belittled	Hurt	Stressed
Betrayal	Hysterical	Stupid
Bitter	Impure	Suffocated
Blamed	Inadequate	Suicidal
Can't do anything right	Inferior	Thwarted
Can't trust anyone	Insecure	Torn apart
Cheap	Insensitive to my needs	Trapped
Cheated	Insignificant	Trash
Condemned	Invalidated	Ugly
Confused	Left out	Unable to communicate
Conspired against	Lied to	Unaccepted
Controlled	Lonely	Uncaring
Cut off	Lost	Uncared for
Deceived	Made fun of	Un-chosen
Defeated	Manipulated	Unclean
Defenseless	Mindless	Unfairly judged
Defrauded	Mistreated	Unfairly treated
Degraded	Misunderstood	Unfit
Desires were rejected	Molested	Unimportant
Despair	Neglected	Un-loveable
Destroyed	No good	Unloved
Devalued	Not affirmed	Unnecessary
Didn't belong	Not cared for	Unprotected
Didn't measure up	Not cherished	Unsafe

Dirty	Not deserving to live	Unsympathetic
Disappointed	Not listened to	Unwanted
Disgusted	Not measure up	Used
Disrespected	Not valued	Violated
Dominated	Opinions not valued	Vulnerable
Embarrassed	Out of control	Wasted
Empty	Overwhelmed	Wicked
Exposed	Pathetic	Worthless
Failure	Pressure to perform	Fear

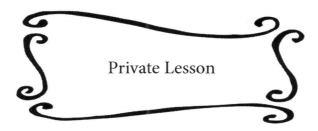

Private Lesson

Ask God to direct your discussion to the areas and issues you need to discuss.

Take turns asking each other these questions. Listen well. Try to understand what the pain did to your mate's heart. Provide a safe haven for him or her to wrestle with any bitterness. Remember, you can't fix it for them.

Do you struggle with bitterness? Do you have someone who is difficult for you to forgive?

What caused the bitterness? How did the incident make you feel? Use the Emotional Pain Words on the previous pages to help you. Be as specific as possible and write the emotion in the space below.

When someone treats you in the same way, do you get angry? Do you hide? Do you indulge in something as a way of "medicating the pain"?

Do you ever get angry or frustrated with me because I've made you feel that way?

If a person or situation surfaced, ask your spouse if they are willing to work through the forgiveness process described earlier in this session. Offer to pray with and support your spouse if they need to forgive someone who has hurt them. Tell them you want them to get out of the torture chamber (Matthew 18:35) and enter God's freedom.

Ask God to help you resolve any problem areas.

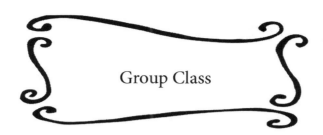

Group Class

1. Hebrews 12:15 says that a root of bitterness "causes all kinds of trouble." Have you ever had a tree root "cause all kinds of trouble"? Discuss and explain the analogy.

2. If someone has hurt you deeply, explain how that might interfere with your relationship with your spouse and with others.

3. Why would forgiving another person in your past improve your marriage?

4. How would you go about forgiving someone who hurt you so badly you really don't want to forgive them?

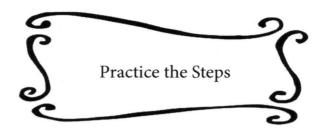

Practice the Steps

1. Resolve to forgive people who have sinned against you.

2. Keep praying to "forgive from the heart" until you are free.

3. Ask God to show you what you should ask forgiveness for since you don't want to be a stumbling block to someone else.

4. _____

5. _____

Session 6

Sin: Pride

Chapter 7B, pages 97-100 from *The Marriage Dance*
For a better understanding of this topic, we suggest you read the full chapter.

We will spend three weeks on chapter 7.

Pride is an exalted view of yourself that is expressed in thoughts, attitudes, words, and actions. It is selfish. It involves a desire to control. Pride is the sin that caused Satan to fall (Isaiah 14:12-14 and Ezekiel 28:12-17). Pride caused Adam and Eve to put what they thought was best ahead of God's clear instructions.

Imagine two dancers whose goal is to make themselves look good even at the expense of their partner. This will not create a smooth, harmonious dance. It definitely will not create a smooth, harmonious marriage either. Imagine marriage partners who try to control to get their way. They will never experience the gift of giving love, and their mate will likely tire of their selfish, controlling attitude. The best harmony is achieved when both partners give generously.

Types of Pride
The type of pride we usually think of is arrogance. It is self-centered. Proud people focus on themselves, their achievements, and their possessions. They always want their way. An arrogant person talks about himself or herself a lot. They rarely ask their spouse how he or she feels. They put their choices about purchases, restaurants, and movies ahead of their spouse's. They ignore or overlook their mate's feelings. They control the situation. An arrogant person is usually blind to how his or her pride affects others and blind to how others see it.

Pride is also self-protection. Many of our self-generated strategies are born out of fear. God wants us to move from reacting out of fear to initiating out of love.

There is another form of pride – hidden pride. This kind of pride still focuses on self, but it is subtle and doesn't appear arrogant. Hidden pride is often a result of inner pain or rejection so it may surface as self-pity. The person is still selfish and wants everything his or her way. They may make excuses so that what they want becomes the only viable option. They may complain which keeps everyone focused on them. This person seldom shows love to others because he or she is consumed with his or her feelings. He or she might not mind keeping everyone waiting while attending to personal needs. The person suffering from hidden pride also seeks to control the situation but does it with quiet manipulation rather than domination. By withdrawing and building walls, the person with hidden pride tries to protect self from further pain.

Examples of Hidden Pride

John Regier of *Biblical Concepts in Counseling* gives these examples: A desire to be recognized and appreciated, hurt feelings when others are promoted but you are overlooked, focus on yourself rather than others, blaming others for their failures, becoming defensive when criticized, being concerned about what others think of you, difficulty in admitting when you have failed another person, viewing others as lower than yourself, wanting others to meet your needs, wanting self-advancement, trying to be successful apart from God's blessing or direction, refusing to give up personal rights, wanting to control others, talking about yourself all the time, drawing attention to your abilities and achievements, feeling sorry for yourself because you're not appreciated, focusing on your knowledge and experience, developing a self-sufficient attitude, and excluding God or others.

The Solution

Here is the solution to pride: "You shall love the Lord your God with all your heart, and with all your soul, and with all your mind. The second [command] is like it, you shall love your neighbor as yourself" (Matthew 22:37, 39, 40). We need to put the focus on God and our partner, not ourselves. A sample prayer might be: "Lord, I admit that I have been putting myself first. I need your help to give preference to You and others—especially my spouse."

The marriage dance involves making a decision to be on the same team as your spouse, as well as working to speak to your spouse's heart. If you have done both of those things, your spouse may be a good person to ask if you have pride. Be ready to listen to and accept his or her loving input.

Improve Your Technique

Write Philippians 2:3 in your words.

Ask God if you put yourself ahead of your spouse? How?

Ask God if you are guilty of hidden pride by focusing primarily on your needs and feelings. List the ways below.

Ask God if you manipulate to get your way? Do you like to control the situation?

Ask God if you pity yourself or complain. Write the situations here.

When you are ready, pray a prayer like this one:

> "Lord, I realize I am doing things my way and not Your way. An example of this is [_____]. Please forgive me. I choose to do things Your way in the future. Please help me."

Private Lesson

Ask God to direct your discussion to the areas and issues you need to discuss.

Take turns sharing some of the things God showed you this week. Now is a good time to practice speaking to each other's heart. Listen intently to what your spouse has to say. Try to understand the feelings that go with the words. Make a safe, supportive place for each other to share.

If you feel you have the freedom to do so, ask your spouse if they think you struggle with pride. You should only ask if you want to know the answer so you can change and have a better marriage.

Ask your spouse if he or she feels there are some ways you do not show them preference. (Listen carefully and do not be defensive.)

Ask God to help you resolve any problem areas.

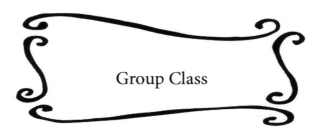

Group Class

1. What was most helpful to you in the discussion about pride?

2. Think of someone who is arrogantly proud. Describe what makes you think they're arrogant.

3. Describe someone you think has hidden pride. How does it show itself?

4. What ways did you spot that you put yourself first in your marriage? In other areas?

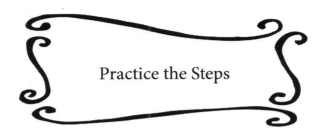

Practice the Steps

What steps should you start practicing this week?

1. Identify examples where you put your desires before others.

2. _____

3. _____

Session 7

Sin: Rebellion, Craving Things that Don't Last, Sexual Sins, Hypocrisy

Chapter 7C, pages 100-110 from *The Marriage Dance*
For a better understanding of this topic, read the full chapter.

Because sins wreak havoc in our marriages and our relationships, we are covering Chapter 7 of The Marriage Dance in three sessions.

Session 7C summarizes

Rebellion

Craving Things that Don't Last

Sexual Sins

Hypocrisy

Rebellion

Rebellion is intentional disobedience of valid authority– parents, employers, the government, God. A rebellious person thinks he or she knows best and decides for themselves regardless of the consequences. Rebels push back against authority and anyone who reminds them of authority. They can think the authority over them is unfair and feel justified in their rebellion. In 1 Samuel 15:1-35, King Saul disobeys God's explicit instructions. God called it rebellion. Whereas pride is putting ourselves first, rebellion is disobeying legitimate authority to do what we want to do.

There is also a less obvious form of rebellion. The passive or "hidden" rebel doesn't get in your face. Rather, he says he'll do something knowing that he won't do it. As in the story of the two brothers in Matthew 21:28-32, the disobedient brother's words are cooperative, but his actions are rebellious. He sabotages the assignment without saying anything hostile.

Whether rebellion is overt or passive, it causes a problem in marriage. Overt rebels won't be told what to do. Passive rebels won't either, but they don't tell their partners that they are resisting. If one or both partners constantly resist, moving as one is impossible. Imagine a rebel who refuses to stay within an agreed-upon budget or a spouse who won't be constrained to let his or her partner know they will be coming home late. The rebellion can easily lead to fear, mistrust, and an attempt by the other spouse to rein in the out-of-control situation.

The solution to rebellion is submission to the authority over you. Here is a sample prayer: "Lord, have I been rebellious – (either openly or passively)? I admit I have been rebellious to both You and others. From now on I want to respond with an open heart and a Christ-like attitude toward each authority you have placed over me." Ask God to show you when you have been rebellious. If God brings a person or situation to mind, acknowledge it specifically and ask God's forgiveness.

When marriage and personal problems seem unresolvable, go back to the areas of bitterness, pride, and rebellion. Ask God whether you have thoroughly resolved these issues.

Craving Things That Don't Last

Craving things that don't last means putting emphasis on what you can buy, acquire, eat, or attain. We usually think of money and greed, but the problem goes beyond greed to seeking success, status, prestige, career, fame, position, even an overabundance of personal goals or entertainment to the exclusion of the things that will last forever. God cares about people because they are eternal. He does not give priority to things that don't last. (Matthew 6:19-21)

Jesus told us that we could not serve two masters (Matthew 6:24). Making outward possessions our master distracts us from serving God. The same can be true in your marriage. If you are too busy with assets, you cannot focus on your mate or spiritual realities.

In dance, you can add costumes, makeup, and accessories, but if they take precedence over dancing well, you still don't have a good dance. The trappings of showmanship will become a distraction. In the same way, focusing on outward cravings will cause problems in your marriage. One spouse spends too much causing the other one to feel angry or insecure. One partner works such long hours that the other feels unloved.

Paul found the answer in an attitude of contentment. "I have learned to be content in whatever circumstances I am. I know how to get along with humble means, and I also know how to live in prosperity; in any and every circumstance I have learned the secret of being filled and going hungry, both of having abundance and suffering need" (Philippians 4:11,12).

Pray a prayer like this: "Lord, I have placed a higher value on [name the items or goals] to the neglect of my relationship with You and others. I want to make You first in my life and establish priorities that honor You and count for eternity. I ask Your forgiveness, and I commit to prioritizing my relationship with You and others above [the things that will not last]."

Sexual Sins

God has a design for marriage. His plan is one of purity and commitment to one man or one woman for life. Anything that defaces, disfigures, or desecrates this design is sexual sin. Sexual sin affects the marriage relationship both before the wedding and during the marriage. God's Word is quite clear in this area. (Exodus 20:14; Deuteronomy 5:18; 1 Thessalonians 4:3-8; 1 Corinthians 6:15-20; Ephesians 4:17-19; Matthew 5:28)

Sexual sins destroy the emotional intimacy that a committed marriage can create. When one spouse forms a sexual bond with someone else, he or she not only breaks the seventh commandment about the sin of adultery, the trust and openness between the two marriage partners are destroyed. The cheating partner becomes secretive and can no longer share his or her heart. The cheated spouse senses the loss of intimacy and closes down as well. The bond between the two is broken.

Similarly, when the couple engages in premarital sex, suspicion and insecurity lie just beneath the surface of the relationship. A wife wonders, "If he didn't need to commit to me before marriage to join in a sexual bond, he might just as easily have an affair with someone else now."

This principle holds true even if the "other woman" takes the form of a video or photograph. Pornography is a fraud; it distorts God's design. It is not reality. The faithful partner feels cheated. The cheating spouse senses the partner pushing them away and feels less fulfilled than before.

Sometimes sexual sins are a symptom of a deeper problem in men who may have wounds or feelings of inadequacy that cause sexual dysfunction. Men may substitute the pleasurable feeling of sex for the less pleasurable feelings of inadequacy, bitterness, and other negative emotions. If you are struggling in this area, you are not alone. If you have a current problem with pornography, there is hope for you, but it will not be easy. Seek out another spiritually mature man who has conquered this area and let him work with you in gaining freedom.

Any activity that doesn't contribute to the purity and sanctity of marriage takes away from it. Some examples of sexual sins: Lust (toward the same or opposite sex), viewing pornography, masturbation, homosexuality or lesbian activity, sexual arousal of another who is not your spouse, premarital sexual relationships, adultery, exposing yourself, sexual harassment, incest, sexual abuse, rape, abortion (either had an abortion or got a woman pregnant who then had an abortion), bestiality, prostitution, going to topless or nude bars, participating in cyber-sex or phone sex, wife swapping.

Past failures can't be undone, but repentance brings the freedom of God's forgiveness. Ask God to remind you of each time you violated His design. From the heart, admit you were wrong for each one. Ask Him to forgive you. You might pray like this: "Lord, I am guilty of violating Your design for marriage by [say what you did and with whom]. I feel guilty and ashamed. It distances me from You. I allowed Satan to gain a foothold in my life. I know my sin has caused repercussions in my marriage. I am sorry for my sin. Please forgive me. Wash me. Free me from each sin and take back the ground I turned over to Satan.

Suggestions for gaining freedom from habitual sexual sin or pornographic photos:

1. Repent deeply with prayer. Holy Spirit-driven guilt is different than Satan inspired shame. When tempted, pray, "Lord, I want to do things your way. I want to rejoice in the partner you've given me (Proverbs 5:18). Help me."

2. Re-program your mind by memorizing Scripture. Meditate on verses about freedom, love and life. Find a relevant passage of Scripture, memorize it, and recite it as long as the temptation exists. See Scriptural suggestions below.

3. The *Conquer* series featuring Ted Roberts and others is an excellent aid in gaining freedom in this area (http://www.conquerseries.com). Join a small group with a leader who has freedom.

4. Don't stay in denial. Put on the belt of truth. Admit you have a problem (Ephesians 6:14).

5. Secrecy is Satan's weapon. Go to someone who can help. Find an accountability partner of your own sex whom you trust who has conquered this area until you are free.

6. Pursue freedom from your emotional wounds. Many times, sexual addiction is a means of medicating your emotional pain.

7. Journal and determine what triggers your acting out. Avoid or prepare for those triggers.

8. Flee temptation (II Timothy 2:22).

9. Don't live in the world of fantasy. Live in the world of reality. Develop real relationships with God, your spouse, and real people.

10. Avoid bad company which corrupts good morals (I Corinthians 15:33).

Scriptures for Meditation

Scriptures Regarding Freedom from Sin

"It was for freedom that Christ set us free" (Galatians 5:1). Psalm 1; Psalm 119:11; Isaiah 61:1-3; John 8:31-32, 44; John 15:1-17; 1 Thessalonians 4:1-8; Romans 6-8; Romans 13:11-14; 1 Corinthians 6:18-20; 1 Corinthians 9:24-27; 2 Corinthians 10:3-5; Galatians 5:13,14; Galatians 5:19-22; Ephesians 6:10-19; Philippians 2:1-8; Philippians 4:5-8; 1 Thessalonians 5:5-8; Romans 14:17; 2 Timothy 1:7; 2 Timothy 2:22; Hebrews 12:1-11; James 1:12-15.

Scriptures Regarding Love

"There is no fear in love, but perfect love casts out fear" (1 John 4:18). Matthew 22: 35-40; 1 Corinthians 13; Matthew 5:43-46; Luke 6:27-35; Luke 16:13; John 3:16; John 13: 34, 35; John 14:15-31; John 17:20-26; John 21:15- 19; Romans 12:10; Romans 13:8-10; 1 Corinthians 2:9; 1 Corinthians 8:1; 1 Corinthians 16:14; 2 Corinthians 5:14,15; Ephesians 3:17-19; Colossians 3:14; Colossians 3:19; 1 Thessalonians 3:12; 2 Thessalonians 3:5; 1 Timothy 1:5; 1 Timothy 4:12; Hebrews 10:24-25; James 2:8; 1 Peter 1:22; 1 Peter 4:8; 2 Peter 1:3-8; 1 John 2:7-14; 1 John 3:10-18; 1 John 3:23; 1 John 4:16-19; 1 John 5:1-5.

Scriptures Regarding Life

John 4: 13-14; John 6:63; John 7:37,38; John 8:12; John 10:7-11; 11:25-26; Matthew 10:39; Romans 5:17-21; Romans 6:22-23; Romans 8:1-11; Galatians 2:20; 6:8; 1 Timothy 4:8; James 1:12; 1 John 5:11-13.

Hypocrisy

Originally, the word "hypocrite" meant an actor in a Greek play. The actor put on a mask and played a role. Today's connotation of the word is presenting yourself as someone you are not or requiring someone else to do something you are not willing to do.

Another possibility is that you conceal part of yourself because you are afraid to tell people who you are. You smile and nod even when you disagree. You hide your true thoughts. As long as you prevent others from knowing you fully, you prevent them from loving you fully. When you put up a façade for others to see, you never know whether they love you or your false front. This includes your spouse who doesn't know you because you give inconsistent and inaccurate signals. Whether the hypocrisy is intentional or unintentional, it is dishonest. If one spouse conceals his or her struggles—or joys—the other spouse cannot nurture or connect. A balanced partnership cannot be built on hypocrisy and on concealing who you are.

In Matthew 23:13-29, Jesus took a dim view of hypocrites, pointing out how their actions were aimed at making themselves look good—often at others' expense. While they looked good on the outside, they were dead on the inside. You can imagine how troubling it would be to marry someone who constantly elevated themselves by diminishing you or who pasted their happy face on when they went to church but then came home and grumbled all week.

Hypocrisy takes many forms:

- Agreeing to perform a task with no intention of actually doing it

- Criticizing others when you have the same problem

- Disguising your bitterness toward others while pretending to love them

- Saying one thing while believing another

- Concealing your weaknesses for fear of rejection

- Hiding activities you are ashamed of

- Making a show of religiosity

- Performing to win approval rather than please God

The solution to hypocrisy is a decision to be real, to let go of hiding, and to be authentic. Ask God to help you. Pray, "Father, please reveal the areas in which I have been a hypocrite. Show me how I hide my real identity. I want to be transparent and real with people--especially my spouse."

Get Rid of Baggage

You may have noticed some of these sins are evident in your spouse. You may be the best person to help him or her address these areas—but only after you've attended to your own sins. (Matthew 7:1-5) Get rid of your baggage first and see how much better you can dance. Then, offer to help your spouse. If he or she accepts your offer, come to the task with an attitude of humility, a desire to see your spouse set free, and a vision of the two of you creating a beautiful dance.

It is popular to blame bad communication for marriage problems. However, not all problems are communication problems. Often the root of a problem is the sin we bring into the marriage. These sins cause problems when we communicate so we think they are communication problems.

Our list of sins is not exhaustive, but it is amazing how many relationship problems are resolved by addressing these six areas. When you find yourself stepping on each other's toes, start with this checklist.

Ask God to reveal how sin has gotten in the way of the dance He designed for your marriage. Then ask him to forgive you and commit to following His way from now on. God wants your freedom more than you want it.

Improve Your Technique

Begin your personal study with prayer. Pray for yourself, asking God to show you how committed you are to having a great marriage.

Lord, what problem areas has my marriage revealed? (For example anger, selfishness, self-focus, rebellion, a tendency to hide, a focus on things that won't matter in 10 years, sexual sins.)

Lord, is there something I did wrong in the past that is still causing problems? What is it?

Lord, how have my sins hurt my marriage?
Listen carefully. Write anything God brings to mind.

Am I willing to address the root problems honestly and thoroughly? Will I take steps to change if God reveals a change of direction I must take?

Pray for your spouse as God leads him or her to deal with problem areas. Write a prayer here.

Rebellion

Pray: "Lord, am I rebellious?" If He says you are, is it an in-your-face rebellion or a quiet, passive rebellion?

Ask God if there is a particular area in which you don't want to be told what to do? Why is that?

When you are ready, pray a prayer like this one:

> "Lord, I have had a rebellious attitude toward authority You
> have placed over me. In the past, I have responded by
> [_____]. Please forgive my rebellious
> attitude. Help me submit to proper authority in the future."

Craving Things That Don't Last

Write these verses in your words.

Matthew 6:24

Philippians 4:11-12

Ask God if there are areas you give more importance than your relationship with God and others? (For example career, money, possessions, position, sports or hobbies, TV, video games, surfing the Internet, personal goals). Write your answer here.

Ask God if these poor priorities have impacted your marriage and family. Write your answer here.

Bonus Question: Read the book of Ecclesiastes. What did Solomon crave? What would be comparable today? How did it affect him? What did Solomon see as the result?

If you have placed the temporal ahead of God and your marriage, pray,

"Lord, I admit I have placed a higher value on _____ to the neglect of my relationship with You and others. I ask Your forgiveness, and I make a commitment to value my relationship with You and others above_____."

Sexual Sins

Summarize each of the following passages.

1 Thessalonians 4:3-8

1 Corinthians 6:15-20

Ephesians 4:17-19

Matthew 5:28

Ask God if you have violated any of His principles regarding sexual purity. Write what you hear the Holy Spirit saying to you in the space below.

Ask God if your sexual struggles are a symptom of a deeper problem. What triggers these struggles? Are they caused by a sense of inadequacy or uncertainty that reflects a deeper problem?

Ask God to remind you of each time you violated His design for marriage. From the heart, admit your sin in each one. Ask God to forgive you.

Memorize, meditate on, and quote the Scriptures found on page 94 when you are tempted.

Find an accountability partner of your sex. Write the name in the space below. Contact the person and ask if he or she will hold you accountable in your quest for freedom.

When you are ready, pray a prayer similar to this.

> "Lord, I admit and reject my sinful involvement in_____
> with_____and ask you to break that stronghold in my life.
> My sin allowed Satan to take control of part of my life. I ask you, Lord
> Jesus, to help me take it back because I want to give You control of all of
> my life."

Hypocrisy

Read Matthew 23 to see what Jesus had to say about hypocrisy. Now write these verses in your words:

1 Peter 2:1

Luke 12:2-3

Ask God if you are a hypocrite. Ask Him to reveal the areas. Ask Him to show you how you hide your real identity.

Tell God you would like to be transparent and real with people especially your spouse. Then ask Him to show you if you hide because you are afraid of something. Ask Him to reveal your fear.

Ask God how your hypocrisy affects your marriage. Write His answer here.

When you are ready, pray a prayer like this one,

"Lord, I admit my hypocrisy as evidenced through my_____. I ask your forgiveness because I want to change. Help me always to be open, truthful, and honest from my heart."

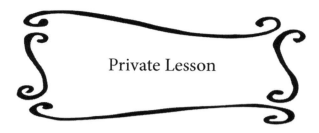

Private Lesson

Ask God to direct your discussion to the areas and issues you need to discuss.

1. Take turns sharing some of the insights that God showed you this week. This is a good time to practice speaking to each other's heart. Listen intently to what your spouse has to say. Try to understand the feelings that go with the words. Make a safe, supportive place for each other to share.

2. Describe how you feel about sharing deeply personal spiritual matters with each other. Begin praying that the Holy Spirit will help you change this area in your life and marriage.

3. If you feel you have the freedom to do so, ask your spouse if they think you struggle with any of the sins covered in the last three sessions. (bitterness, pride, rebellion, craving things that don't last, sexual sins, hypocrisy). You should only ask if you want to know the answer to change and have a better marriage. Make sure both of you have "taken the log out of your own eye" before asking your spouse about the speck in his or her eye (Matthew 7:1-5).

Ask God to help you resolve any problem areas.

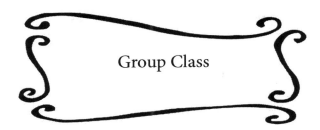

Group Class

1. Did the definitions of any of the sins surprise you? Which ones?

2. What caught your attention?

3. What was most helpful to you?

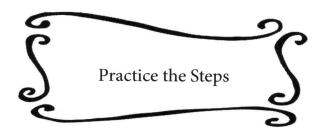

Practice the Steps

Ask God to point out the areas you need to turn over to Him.

1. _____

2. _____

3. _____

Wounds: Everyone is Wounded

Chapter 8, pages 111-125 from *The Marriage Dance*
For a better understanding of this topic, we suggest you read the full chapter.

Most of us learn to compensate for the emotional hurts we received early in life. The wounds are still there, but we learn how to obscure them and function in everyday society. The problem arises when two people with unhealed wounds marry. Inevitably, they will "step on each other's toes" with the resultant "ouch-ing" and striking back or pulling away from each other or refusing to "dance" anymore. Marriage does not cause the original wounds; it merely reveals them. The pain can persist without either spouse understanding what is driving it. Until the original pain is resolved, any solution will be a temporary surface agreement, and the disappointments will reoccur.

Unresolved Wounds
You do not need to go looking for your wounds. If they are there, they will find you. Instead, be open and willing to ask God if there are unresolved problem areas in your life. Jesus wants to heal our wounds. If the same problem keeps emerging in your marriage— if you keep exploding (either outwardly or inwardly) when similar situations present themselves, you must look to see if you have an unresolved wound. If you avoid discussing a particular topic, you may have a wound. Suppressing unruly emotions does not help. Refusing to acknowledge you have a wound does not make it go away. Those tactics would be tantamount to entering a dance competition with a broken leg. Either you or your partner is going to get hurt—probably both of you. At a minimum, you are unlikely to have a winning dance.

Consequences
There are consequences for not tending to wounds. First, the same problems keep returning. You explode when you feel trapped; you withdraw when you feel ignored. Second, you risk passing some damage down to your children. The wound of losing a parent early in your life may cause you to cling to your children causing them to run for

the hills as soon as they are able. Third, wounds hinder your ability to give love to your spouse freely and to receive it from them. In an attempt to protect yourself from getting hurt again, you shutter your heart.

FOUR TYPES OF WOUNDS

Type of Wound	Possible Causes	Possible Consequences
Physical	A parent who disciplines too harshly or inappropriately. Physical abuse from a sibling, school bully, or spouse.	Anger, bitterness, hopelessness. Walls that create emotional distance.
Emotional	Placing excessively high expectations on a child. Forcing child to assume adult responsibilities when they are still too young. Child feels he must mediate his parents' fights. Hurtful words. Neglect.	Feeling hopeless about meeting expectations or goals. Feeling like everything depends on you. A broken spirit. Feeling trapped.
Sexual	Inappropriate touching, molestation, rape, the aggressor exposing himself or herself or showing the victim pornography.	Becoming dominant or controlling in an attempt to prevent future abuse. Distrust. Keeping people at a distance. Guilt. Shame.
Spiritual	Forcing church or spirituality on someone. Legalism without love or with hypocrisy. Forced involvement in a cult.	Bitterness. Anger. Rebellion against biblical principles or God. Unwillingness to trust God. Belief that God is harsh and unloving. Difficulty praying.

If wounds are left unhealed, you will not be able to give and/or receive love freely, and you will impact those close to you, especially your mate.

It is possible to believe one thing in your head and another in your heart. What you believe in your heart will dictate how you live your life and what you do. For example, you may believe in your head that God will never leave you or forsake you (Hebrews 13:5, Deuteronomy 31:8, Joshua 1:5). However, if you found yourself in a precarious situation and felt God did not come to your rescue, you may believe in your heart that God does not always make good on His promises—at least not for you. The actions then follow: "If God is not going to take care of me, I guess I'd better take care of myself."

Numbed Heart

Another problem is not allowing your heart to feel at all. Doctors, soldiers, and policemen need to keep their emotions in check so they can perform their jobs effectively. Engineers and lawyers may dwell so much in the intellectual world that their emotions get lost.

Whether your emotions got locked away through a wound, or by consciously suppressing them or through lack of use, you still have a problem. When you get home to your spouse and loved ones, they need all of you—including fully functioning emotions—including a heart that can give and receive love.

The more unresolved wounds you bring to your marriage, the more opportunities to step on each other's toes. If you have a strong emotional reaction or if you keep bumping into the same argument or uncomfortable situation, ask God if you have an underlying wound. Don't look for problems that don't exist or dwell on non-problems, but if the same emotion or problem keeps affecting your marriage, there's a reason.

Dealing with Wounds

Dealing with wounds gets more difficult when your wound collides with your mate's wound. In essence, you are "stepping on each other's toes." It is difficult to love and focus on your mate while he or she is hurting you. One party must be willing to put his or her needs on hold and address the other's wound.

Dealing with sins that block relationships is fairly straightforward. On the other hand, it is harder to deal with wounds since each person's wounds are unique. Are you willing to ask God to begin healing your wounds? When you take responsibility for the over-reactions and emotional disruptions you are causing in your marriage, many of the problems will go away.

Do you believe you have wounds that affect you today? Do you have sensitive areas or arguments that keep recurring in your life? Consider that you might have a festering wound that needs to be healed.

4 SIGNS OF WOUNDEDNESS

How would you know if you have been wounded? Four signs of woundedness are listed below. Ask God to show you if any of these problems are present in your life. If He brings something to mind, write down the specifics.

1. Negative Thought Patterns (The same negative thought keeps playing in your mind.)

2. Recurring Problems

3. Out-of-proportion Emotional Reactions

4. Self-Protection

Improve Your Technique

"The Spirit of the Lord is upon me, because He anointed me to preach the gospel to the poor: He has sent me to proclaim release to the captives, and recovery of sight to the blind, to set free those who are oppressed." Luke 4:18 (Also see Isaiah 61:1-2.)

"Surely our griefs He Himself bore, and our sorrows He carried."
Isaiah 53:4

Jesus came to release you so you no longer have to be a captive and so you will see from his viewpoint. Did He come to set you free from your oppression and to take on your grief and sorrow? How does He do this for you?

Look up these verses: John 8:32, John 10:10, and Galatians 5:1. What promise does God make to you?

Do you have recurring problems that cause you to react out-of-proportion to the problem?

What provokes or triggers those reactions?

How do you deal with your reactions (control, hide, indulge, or try to be perfect)?

EMOTIONAL, PHYSICAL, SPIRITUAL, AND SEXUAL WOUNDS

List each person who wounded you, how you were wounded, and the emotional pain it caused.

Who caused the wound?	Describe the incident	What pain did it cause?	Identify the emotion. Refer to Emotional Pain Words chart. (Pages 77-78)

Pray this prayer.

"Lord, I admit but reject the harm (<u>name of person</u>) caused me. This pain has become a stronghold in my life, and I ask You to break it. I ask You, Lord Jesus, to take back any ground I gave to the enemy, and I yield that ground to Your control.

"Lord, I choose to forgive (<u>name of person</u>) for (incident) causing me to feel (<u>describe emotion</u>), and I ask you, Jesus, to take the pain away. I also choose to yield to Your way in my life, believing You know what is best for me."

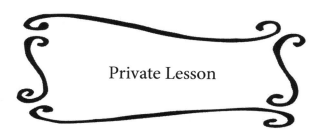

Private Lesson

Ask God to direct your discussion to the areas and issues you need to discuss.

If you feel safe, ask your spouse to help you explore the questions above. Then consider these questions for your private lesson.

Do you have arguments in which you both react badly?

How does your spouse hurt you and your response hurt your spouse at the same time? (Also known as "stepping on the other's toes.") Make a list and add to it as you see new areas. Ask God for wisdom on how to handle these issues.

If you identified a topic, a fear, or a disagreement where you react, control, hide, run away, or strike out in anger and it still affects you, share it with your spouse.

Use this time to learn more about the people and incidents that made your spouse the way he or she is. What is he or she afraid of? Listen carefully to the words and watch for the non-verbal clues as to how he or she feels. Ask questions such as, "Does that still affect you today?" "If so, how?" "Do I sometimes make you feel that same way?" Make sure your spouse knows that it is safe to share with you. Try to understand what happened and the hurt he or she felt. Some people can no longer remember the specific incident. That's okay. Just identify the tender spots where it is not safe to go.

If you feel safe doing so, discuss the areas in your marriage where problems seem to reoccur. (Topics such as sex or money, situations such as visiting family or getting ready to leave the house). How do you *feel* when those topics or situations come up? Be as specific as possible. We will cover how to resolve these topics and situations in a later session. This is not a time to defend yourself. Just put the areas on the table and begin praying that God will help you understand the root of the problem and His solution to it.

Ask God to help you resolve any problem areas.

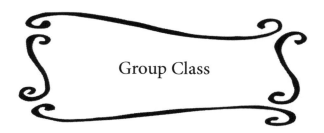

Group Class

1. What questions do you have?

2. What caught your attention?

3. What did you learn about God, yourself, or your spouse?

4. What did you realize you need to be practicing?

5. How did you put the steps/information into practice this week?

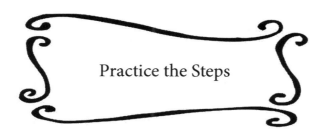

Practice the Steps

Start a list. What are the problems that keep reoccurring in your marriage?
Add to the list.

1. _____

2. _____

3. _____

Session 9

Wounds: Beware Your Reaction

Chapter 9, pages 126-136 from *The Marriage Dance*
For a better understanding of this topic, we suggest you read the full chapter.

Bad things happen to everyone. We are injured by someone else's wrong decisions or actions. We have a stillborn child. And so many other life situations. While we are not responsible for the wound, we are responsible for our reactions to it. Sometimes we get bitter toward the other person or we blame God or assume wrong facts about His character. We may blame our family or friends for letting us down. We may blame ourselves.

The Enemy's Role
The devil is the Deceiver-in-Chief. He delights in taking a painful event, feeding you a wrong interpretation of it and getting you to believe it. Or, he tells you a half-truth. The part about the pain is real, so it is very easy to believe the wrong interpretation of the event. For example, let's say you are dealing with a chronic disease. The disease is true. It happened. However, the devil points out that God could heal you if He wanted to. Therefore, God must not be a good or loving god. Or, God must not love you enough to heal you. The conclusions are not true—but, in the midst of your pain, they may seem true. You then proceed to live your life as though you are dealing with a god who does not love you—even if you came to your conclusion subconsciously.

Think about the painful events in your life. Have you come to some wrong conclusions based on them? Satan doesn't have any new tricks. His half-truths and aspersions on God's character go back to the Garden of Eden when he implied God didn't want Adam and Eve to eat the forbidden fruit because He was withholding good from them. The knowledge of good and evil must be something good, and God was preventing them from possessing this knowledge. You see his same tricks in the story of Job's loss and in Jesus' temptation in the wilderness. Unlike Adam and Eve, Job and Jesus did not buy the lie.

We make decisions based upon what we think an event meant. If God didn't send anyone to my aid, it must mean He has more important priorities than me. If I was ignored, it must be because I am insignificant.

Believing the Lie

We want the pain to stop. Our thinking is confused. We base our perception of reality in that moment. Logic, rational discourse, objective thinking, and Bible reading are given low priority. We react out of pain, frustration, exhaustion, anger, hurt, fear and the voices in our head telling us what is true. We believe a lie because it seems so true and we desperately want to avoid further pain. We might even make a "vow" like: "I will never allow this to happen again." Have you been there?

We must be careful about making snap interpretations upon which we base future decisions. Our natural instinct is to protect ourselves because God doesn't seem like He's going to. Based upon the strong emotions created by the pain, we hold these newfound "truths" close to our heart and even think they are "self-evident." We then base our lives on those apparent truths. The problem: Satan sneaked in a lie and we didn't even see it. Solomon was right: "As a man believes in his heart, so is he" (Proverbs 23:7).

We then live even more in self-protection mode. Protecting ourselves from someone who threatens physical, emotional, social, or spiritual injury is appropriate as long as we are in danger. But after time elapses and we are no longer in immediate danger, we continue to protect ourselves so the injury will never happen again. We are on guard and also on the defensive. The defense mechanisms remain and surface with those who don't threaten or have any intent to harm—even our spouse.

How We Protect Ourselves

Emotional isolation. We shut down our emotions to avoid having them hurt again. "That was too painful. I'm not going to expose my heart to anyone again." Of course, a shut-down results in you closing your heart to both pain and joy.

Control. We attempt to control the situations, conversations, and people around us. We meter how much information we give out and to whom. We prevent conversations from going in certain directions. We put a noose around our teenagers to make sure they don't have an opportunity to repeat our mistakes. Controlling people tend to be suspicious and untrusting. "I don't want my spouse to have an affair so I will double-check his or her every move."

Hiding. We hide behind a book or a computer screen. We closely guard what we tell others about ourselves or what we are thinking. Women who have been molested may hide behind excess weight. "That was too painful. I will hide so this doesn't happen again."

Indulgence. We make a vain attempt to self-medicate the pain with food, drink, drugs, or a new toy to entertain us. "I don't like the way I'm feeling. I think I'll have a drink—or a Krispy Kreme—or go on a shopping spree."

Perfectionism. We attempt to avoid the pain of being criticized. There is a difference between wanting to do a good job and having to do a good job so you can avoid the pain of criticism. "I'm going to make sure I do a perfect job this time so I won't be criticized again." We project the need to be perfect on to our children.

Notice that all of these actions are attempts at protecting ourselves from further pain. Could you identify with any of them? We don't stop to ask God if He has another plan. In the process, we close ourselves off from those closest to us.

Our self-protective actions will never set us free. John 8:32 tells us: "You will know the truth and the truth will set you free." If we want freedom, we must make the decision to pursue God's truth and act on it.

God's Alternative

God has an alternative: Take Him at His word. Believe God is good and that He loves us and will continue to act in our best interests. Do you believe in His goodness? If you truly believe, your mindset and your actions will be very different than if you believe you must fend for yourself. Are you willing to ask God to show you His plan and to wait for His answer?

The pattern looks like this:

- The painful event happens.

- We interpret the event, usually finding a way to protect ourselves in some way.

- The interpretation may be wrong. It may have been true when the event happened, but not now. It may have been true of the perpetrator, but not true of everyone. It may ignore God's presence or purposes in the event.

- We live our life based upon our interpretation of that event which either consciously or subconsciously affects subsequent decisions.

Improve Your Technique

This section will be very important in transforming both you and your marriage. Make sure you spend the necessary time with it. Pray. Ask God to show you the answers to questions in this section, to identify the events that significantly impacted you, and to clarify your interpretation of those events.

If possible, complete the entire Improve Your Technique section in one day. Go over the same questions again during the rest of the week and record any new insights God gives you.

> "You will know the truth and the truth will make you free."
> John 8:32 NASB

Explain how that verse might apply to some wrong ideas you have unconsciously adopted and now live your life based upon.

Ask God to reveal what events have shaped your perception of the world, of others, and of yourself. Write what you feel here.

List the painful events or reoccurring situations in your life. What do you believe to be true because of these situations? How have these beliefs caused you to act?

Have you been operating on an interpretation of life that is not true?

In what ways do you live on the defensive? In what ways are you afraid of what might happen?

Is there anything you blamed on God instead of looking for Him in it?

Ask God to show you the reason He allowed this painful event to happen to you. Ask Him to show you the situation from His perspective. Write about how you feel.

Is there anything you blame on your family or friends?

Is there anything you blame on yourself?

When you think about these traumatic events or recurring situations, what are your dominant emotions for each one?

Ask the Lord to show you any way you have deceived yourself. Write those here.

Have you shut down your emotions in any situation to avoid criticism? Write about it here.

If you feel hopeless about any situation, ask God to reveal His truth regarding it. Write those truths here.

Sit silently for at least 5 minutes. Ask the Lord to tell you what He thinks of you. Write those descriptions here.

Ephesians 6:16 describes Satan's lies as "flaming arrows." A lie would be something that contradicts what God clearly tells us in the Bible. For example: "I have loved you with an everlasting love" (Jeremiah 31:3). "I will never leave you or forsake you" (Hebrews 13:5). "I can do all things through Christ who strengthens me" (Philippians 4:13).

Are you able to identify some of the lies you have believed? If you need help, ask God to point them out to you. (Read Ephesians 6:16; Jeremiah 31:3; Romans 8:35-39; Hebrews 13:5; Psalm 27:10; Philippians 4:13.)

Do you ever recall making a "vow" that you would never allow your guard down again, would never allow something to happen again? If so, what was it? How did you live life after making that vow?

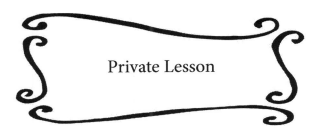

Private Lesson

Ask God to direct your discussion to the areas and issues you need to discuss.

In what ways do I use defensiveness as a crutch?

Do you think it is it easy for me to express love to you? Is it easy for me to receive your love?

What areas do you see where it is difficult for me?

When I get angry, hide, or pretend nothing happened, what has usually triggered those responses?

If you and your spouse are both Christ-followers, ask him or her to share areas where you don't appear to believe what God says about you or God's love for you.

In what specific areas do you see me as motivated by fear? What do you think I am afraid of?

When do I seem to react with emotion that is out of proportion to the situation?

If you remembered making a vow, share it with your spouse and ask if you still appear to be controlled by it.

Ask God to help you resolve any problem areas.

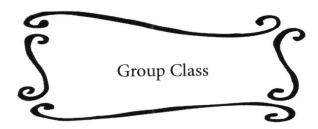

Group Class

1. Were you able to identify any wounds you feel free to share with the group?

2. Did God show you any wrong interpretations of your wounds?

3. Did you identify emotions that surface when you and your mate are having a recurring argument?

4. How did you put the steps/information into practice this week?

5. What do you need to be practicing?

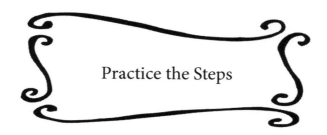

Practice the Steps

What are your action items for this week?

1. _____

2. _____

3. _____

4. _____

What are your requests that you will ask from God?

1. _____

2. _____

3. _____

4. _____

Session 10

Wounds: Resolution of Wounds

Chapter 10 pages 137-151 from *The Marriage Dance*
For a better understanding of this topic, we suggest you read the full chapter.

Following the Improve Your Technique, Private Lesson, and Group Class, you will find a Bonus Section. While it is part of this topic, it may exceed the time you have set aside for completing this section of the workbook. We strongly recommend finding time—either this week or in the coming weeks—to focus on this section as it has the potential to powerfully pull you together as a couple.

Some unhealed wounds may affect your marriage. Here are a few examples:

- A young man whose family did not respect his time and possessions when he was growing up has an outburst of anger whenever he feels his wife disrespects his time and belongings.

- A woman who felt despised and rejected because of her physical appearance still doesn't feel accepted no matter how much her husband demonstrates his love for her.

- A man who felt enormous time pressure from his mother and father interprets every request from his wife as a *demand* to do it now.

- A woman whose friends betrayed her finds it hard to trust anyone including her husband.

- A young wife whose parents closely monitored her feels cornered when her husband asks if she'll be home by dinnertime.

Our emotionally defensive posture prevents our spouse from getting close enough to "dance" with us. We don't want our mate (or anyone else) to get close to our still-open wounds. Christ says He came to heal those wounds. We need to let Him do what he came to do—heal our wounds and set us free.

Confront the Enemy

To follow God's Word, we must confront Satan's subtle lies and hold to the truth. We must let God heal our wounds, love others, stop protecting self, develop a spirit of thankfulness, and have a strong faith that God is always there.

Joseph had a rough time growing up (Genesis 37-50). When he was 17, his ten older brothers despised him so much they threw him into a pit and then sold him to traders going to Egypt. Joseph became the slave of the captain of Pharaoh's bodyguard, Potiphar. Potiphar's wife tried to seduce him and when she failed, she accused him of attempted rape. Though he did nothing wrong, Joseph went from favored son to slave to imprisoned criminal. He was thrown into jail where Joseph met Pharaoh's baker and cupbearer who both were suspected of trying to poison the ruler. Joseph interpreted the two men's dreams and told Pharaoh's cupbearer that he would be restored to his position (which he was) and the baker that he would be killed (which he was). However, when the cupbearer was restored, he forgot his promise to speak well on Joseph's behalf. Before you think through the rest of the famous story, put yourself in Joseph's place. Do you think he thought any of these thoughts?

> "No one, not even my family, loves me."
>
> "No one will help me; everyone is out to take advantage of me."
>
> "Even God has forgotten about me."
>
> "Life is not fair."
>
> "Why should I try so hard? It doesn't do any good."
>
> "Nothing I do ends well."
>
> "This situation is hopeless. I will die in jail."
>
> "God has it in for me."

Those lies may have seemed like truth to Joseph at the time. And like Joseph, many of us believe false statements that resound in our head. Joseph resolved these lies. God was faithful to His Word, and Joseph became great in Pharaoh's house. The trustworthiness of God resolved any doubts Joseph may have had. By the end of the story, his heart was free from bitterness or anger, and he was able to love his brothers. Although Joseph's brothers' intent was evil and Joseph's circumstances were dire, Gods was working behind the scenes and meant it for good from the very start.

130

God's Word Counters These Lies.

"I [God] have loved you with an everlasting love." Jeremiah 31:3

"He [the Lord] is our help and shield." Psalm 33:20

"God causes all things to work together for good to those who love God and are called according to His purpose." Romans 8:28

"I [God] have good plans for you to give you a future and a hope." Jeremiah 29:11

"I [God] will never leave you or forsake you." Hebrews 13:5

"As for you, you meant evil against me, but God meant it for good..." Genesis 50:20

"God sent me before you to preserve for you a remnant in the earth, and to keep you alive by a great deliverance." Genesis 45:7

These words demonstrate that Joseph came to understand the situation from God's point of view. Whether or not Joseph's brothers realized their errors, Joseph had to resolve his wounds and open his heart. God had a plan for Joseph, but it did not include wallowing in pity, bitterly reacting against his brothers, or taking vengeance against them.

Pursuing God's Truth

As we mature in Christ, some wounds seem to resolve themselves. Others require our cooperation in pursuing God's truth.

Make sure you are not merely quoting the relevant verse of Scripture (believing the truth in your head) but that you believe it with every fiber of your being including your emotions.

Ask God if what you believe is true or if you are merely defaulting to a long-held, ingrained lie. For example, "Heavenly Father, I feel as though my husband has been pushing me away all week. Is he pushing me away or is it something else? (Be still and pause to see if God answers.)

Ask God to show you what is causing your feeling.

Ask Him to show you the truth. (Your husband may be concerned about events at work.)

Reiterate the truth every time the wound surfaces. Dwell on the truth. Find a relevant Bible passage and memorize it. Quote it whenever needed.

Don't allow your wounds to fester by pretending there is no conflict or tiptoeing around the delicate subject to avoid the argument. Fighting about it isn't much better. Resolve the issue through prayer and understanding. When you allow God to heal your wounds, you take down the relationship blockades and allow His abundance to come in.

Gaining Freedom—4 Methods

Various Christian authors we studied talk about the lies we believe and how to gain freedom from them.

Method 1

In *Lies Women Believe,* Nancy Leigh DeMoss says we must recognize the devil's lie and apply God's truth. (Remember to make sure you deal with the wounded emotions that are causing the problem and not merely resolving the problem intellectually.)

Method 2

John Regier of *Caring for the Heart Ministries* discusses the negative thought patterns that play like broken records in our brains. After identifying them, he says to engage God in conversational prayer ("God, would you paint a picture of my heart?" "Lord, how do You see me?" "Father, I feel so alone. Is it true that I am alone?" "Jesus, what would you do if I gave you the pain I'm feeling?") and then persist in prayer, waiting until God answers. Count on the fact that God will take His truth and etch it on your heart in a way that will assure you it is from Him. His answer will never contradict what is written in Scripture.

Method 3

Joe Albright, in *Liberating the Bruised,* and James Friesen in, *Uncovering the Mystery of MPD,* do not view the problem as believing a lie, but rather as creating a split personality within ourselves to handle the problem. For example, a person who has been abused may create a "protector" personality within himself. Whenever a threatening situation arises, the strong, assertive protector personality emerges and takes control until the danger passes. Notice that this is still another way of handling the situation on our own rather than turning to God as Jesus always did.

Method 4

Ed Smith of *Theophostic Prayer Ministry* encourages praying these three prayers and patiently waiting for God to answer:

> Lord, what am I feeling?
>
> Lord, when was the earliest time I felt this way?
>
> Lord, what truth and light do you want to shed on this?

Discover which method works best for you. When God heals one wound, ask Him if there is another wound. Pursue His truth and healing. God wants your healing, and one method may work best for you.

13-Point Checklist

1. Recognize that your reaction was out of proportion to the current situation. When feelings are strong and seem appropriate, it isn't easy to see our own over-reaction.

2. Identify the emotion you are feeling. If you need help, refer to a list of emotions such as "Emotional Pain Words" in this workbook and in Appendix A of *The Marriage Dance*. Pick four or five words that describe what you are feeling. Is there a theme? What is the exact emotion?

3. Was there an event earlier in your life when you had that same feeling? Go to the earliest time in your life that you remember feeling that emotion. Ask God to bring the event to mind. Match the emotional feeling. Your emotions will help identify the wound causing this problem.

4. Is there a lie associated with what you believe? Discovering it is tricky. If you knew it was a lie, you wouldn't believe it. It may be a misinterpretation of the event. Ask God to show you where you are out-of-balance in your thinking and to help you discover any deception or pretense in your heart.

5. Ask God to show you the truth of how He sees you. Have a serious personal conversation with God.

   > "God, would you paint me a picture of my heart?"
   >
   > "Lord, how do You see me?"
   >
   > "Father, I feel [insert emotion]."
   >
   > "Jesus, what would you do if I gave you my pain?"
   >
   > "Are my conclusions true?"

6. Once God has shown you the truth, you must choose to believe it experientially. 2 Corinthians 10:4-5 explains that our weapons of warfare are not of this world and that our weapons are capable of demolishing spiritual strongholds—specifically the "speculations and every lofty thing raised up against the knowledge of God." We are instructed to take every thought (the lies) captive to the obedience of Christ. Dwell on what is true, honorable, right, pure, lovely, admirable, excellent,

and praiseworthy (Philippians 4:8-9). For example, if you live under the delusion that you are worthless, take that thought captive and claim the truth that you are "fearfully and wonderfully made" (Psalm 139:14). Pursue this until your heart believes it.

7. Ask God if you reacted wrongly at the time of your wound and need to repent. The sin of others is not your sin, but if someone abused you and you reacted in bitterness, for example, you may need to repent of bitterness. To be free from bitterness you must forgive them from your heart (Matthew 18:35).

8. Ask God if there are any other negative results from the wound or the sin. Hurt is followed by anger and then bitterness. As a result, we shut down our emotions. In addition to working through the bitterness, we must allow God to comfort the pain, and we must learn how to stop suppressing emotions. Though the primary effect of removing bitterness is obvious, there is no freedom until we push through the secondary effects of bottled-up emotions.

9. If you are feeling stuck, ask God to help you resolve the problem. God does not always heal wounds immediately—but He wants to help you. Consider that God may be doing something bigger. He may want to humble you first to test what is in your heart (Deuteronomy 8:2-3). He may allow you to help others who are experiencing a similar situation. It may not be time for Him to reveal His purpose. God did not remind Joseph of his childhood dream for 21 years. Develop a close relationship with Him so that you understand His deeper purposes. Continue a close dialogue with God.

10. Meditate on Scripture. If you struggle with an area where Satan has a foothold, pick a relevant passage of Scripture, memorize it, roll it over and over in your mind throughout the day, and quote it back to Satan when he tempts you. When the devil tempted Jesus in the wilderness, Jesus quoted Scripture.

11. Consider asking a wise Christian counselor or someone with a strong marriage for help. We are often blind to our emotional responses to our wounds.

12. Continue to aggressively eradicate lies. Look for traumatic events you misinterpreted which caused you to question God's goodness and to trust Him less. Also look for long-term patterns which caused you to believe, "That's just

how life is. Nothing will ever change." "I must take control of my own life because I can't trust God to take care of it."

13. Just as the deep emotions of the heart trump your intellect, your will can trump your emotions—but you need courage. If you know the right thing to do, do it—even if your emotions scream "no!" Walk by faith. Eventually, your emotions will follow your will.

There is hope. Praise God for each wound as He heals it. God doesn't allow wounds as a means of punishing us. He allows them to make us more ready for God's Kingdom.

Improve Your Technique

"The Spirit of the Lord is upon Me, because He anointed Me to preach the gospel to the poor. He has sent Me to proclaim release to the captives, and recovery of sight to the blind, to set free those who are oppressed, to proclaim the favorable year of the Lord."
Luke 4:18-21; Isaiah 61:1, 2

List the areas where you are poor, imprisoned, blind, or oppressed. If Jesus were to apply this prophecy to you, what would He do for you?

Write the following verses on a card and carry them with you. If negative thoughts start playing in your head, quote the verses and meditate on their meaning.

"And you will know the truth and the truth will make you free." John 8:32

"It was for freedom that Christ set us free." Galatians 5:1

When God speaks to you, how does he speak? (A verse of Scripture, a thought, a mental picture, the words to a spiritual song, peace in your heart, or some other way?)

On the chart below, record the following answers.

1. What difficult situations, patterns, or recurring events have you had in your life?
2. Ask God if you have any wounds related to those situations, patterns, or events. Write down what He tells or shows you.
3. What message did you take away from those situations? Ask Him if there are any lies you have believed. Write them on the chart. (You will know it is a lie if it contradicts what God has told you in His Word.)
4. Ask God to show you the truth. From God's word, write down the pertinent truth regarding each one.

Difficult Situation or Recurring Events	Resulting Emotional Pain	Lies I Believed	God's Truth (Scripture to meditate on)

Ask God if your wounds have affected your children. If so, how?

What negative thoughts dominate your mind? (For example: "This is hopeless." "I'm stupid." "No one will ever be attracted to me." "I am incompetent." "My friends, parents, siblings don't like me." "God wasn't there when I needed Him." "God never answers my prayers." "I am all alone in this world." "If I need something, I have to get it for myself.")

For each wound you listed above, try these methods for resolving the wounds.

1. Confront the lie with the truth of God's Word as Jesus did in the wilderness. (Matthew 4:1-11; Luke 4:1-13)

2. Engage God in a prayerful conversation using the phrases below. Be sure that you listen for God's response.

    "Lord, how do you see me?"
    "Father, I feel so____. Is it true that I am____?"
    "Lord, were You there when [painful memory] happened?" "Where were You?"
    "Lord, what would You do if I gave this pain to You?" "May I give my pain to You?"

3. Pray these prayers.
    "Lord, what am I feeling?"
    "Lord, when was the earliest time I felt this way?" Go to the earliest source.
    "Lord, what truth and light do you want to shed on this?" What is God's perspective?

4. Pick an issue and work through the 13-point checklist found on pages 133-135.

What is the most important area where you need freedom? How will you pursue freedom with Jesus in that area?

If you have identified a problem, whom can you go to for help? (Jesus, a counselor, your spouse, a friend?)

Of the four methods (page 132) of resolving wounds, which one feels most comfortable to you? Why?

What prevents you from taking the next step into deeper emotional and spiritual relationship? Is there something that makes you fearful or reluctant about resolving old wounds? If so, tell God about it and write a prayer asking for His help.

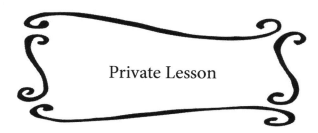

Private Lesson

Ask God to direct your discussion to the areas and issues you need to discuss.

1. Are you both committed to emotional intimacy? If not, what needs to change to get that commitment?

2. Is there a wound in your past that makes you fear emotional intimacy?

3. What are the areas we tiptoe around? List any that come to mind.

4. What are the arguments that repeat themselves in our marriage? Are we committed to getting past these?

5. When has a response been out-of-proportion to the offense? Is it accompanied by a feeling that is connected with a painful memory?

Ask God to help you resolve any problem areas.

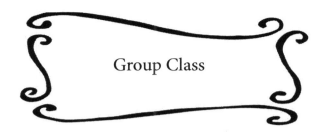

Group Class

1. What caught your attention in this week's homework?

2. What did you learn?

3. What did you realize you need to be practicing?

4. How did you put the steps/information into practice this week?

5. What experiences did you have this week in trying to resolve wounds?

6. What did you learn in the process?

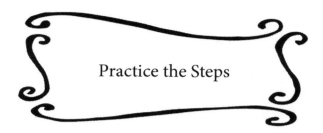

Practice the Steps

Record what you will do this week to implement what you've learned.

1. Throughout the week, fill in the chart regarding difficult situations, emotional pain, lies and God's truth.

2. _____

3. _____

4. _____

Session 10 Bonus

Helping Your Partner Resolve Wounds

This bonus section gives you the opportunity to bring together what you've learned about choosing to be on the same team as your spouse, speaking to your spouse's heart, and resolving sins and wounds that block relationships. We believe this section is very important. If you do not have time to work on it this week, set aside time to go through it at a future time. It is our prayer that this session will bring you to a deeper level of connection than you have ever experienced before.

In Session 1 you learned about embracing your differences as a couple and allowing them to strengthen you as teammates. This bonus exercise will only work if you have committed to being on the same team. If you have, your caring support will be invaluable to your spouse in working through areas that block his or her relationships.

In Session 2 you learned the basics of speaking to your spouse's heart. Hopefully, you have been practicing each week. Not only is this something you perfect through practice, but trust is built through sticking with your spouse through this process and genuinely rooting for his or her freedom.

In Sessions 5, 6, and 7, you studied some sins that notoriously block relationships until they are laid aside. In Sessions 8, 9 and 10 you looked at the people and situations that hurt you deeply and began praying for God to heal and restore those areas.

The remainder of this session focuses on learning to care deeply about the areas that have shaped both you and your spouse and on helping each other work and pray through the resolution of those problem areas.

You can help your spouse take the next step in following God. If your spouse is not yet open to your help, build trust. Show love and respect until he or she is ready. One way to open the door is to allow your spouse to help you get past the sins, wounds, and difficulties of your past. Demonstrate openness to help. If you think you have more maturity in this area, you go first.

Improve Your Technique

Set aside at least 30 minutes with your spouse. The objective will be to help each other through some of the underlying problems that have caused difficulties. In preparation for that time, review your homework for Sessions 5, 6, 7, 8, 9, and 10. Add anything God has shown you since you did the homework for those sessions. Prepare to have your spouse speak to your heart in the areas you have identified and prepare to speak to the heart of your spouse in the areas he or she has identified.

In preparation for speaking to your spouse's heart, answer the following questions.

1. How much do you know about your spouse's early years?

2. What were some of the people and events that gave him or her particular joy?

3. What caused pain, fear, or sadness?

4. What areas particularly bother your spouse?

5. List what you want to know more about.

Begin praying that God will open up the conversation and give you a new level of understanding. Pray that God will give you a listening ear and a caring heart toward your spouse.

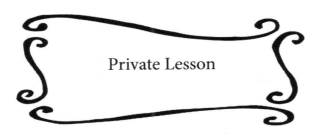

Private Lesson

Your small group may choose to add a week for this Bonus Session in order to provide uninterrupted time for you to complete this exercise or you may complete it with your spouse at home.

Ask God to direct your discussion to the areas and issues you need to discuss.

Couples Breakout

1. Allow at least 30 minutes for this breakout. Use the first 15 minutes for one spouse to ask the questions below, listen carefully, and care deeply. Use the second 15 minutes for the other spouse to do the same.

2. If you have difficulty answering any of the questions, stop to pray. Ask God to show you the answer. A gentle reminder from your spouse can be very helpful. ("Let's take a moment and ask God to show us.") Remember to pause, listening for God's answer.

3. It is more important that you do a thorough job of answering each question than that you make it through all the questions. You can always continue at another time. It is not necessary to take the questions in order.

4. Pray: Start your time together by asking God to open your memory and reveal His truth to you and join the conversation.

5. What feeling or emotion do you still carry from that event or pattern?

6. What was the message that you believed from that event or pattern of events?

7. How have you lived your life based on that belief or message? In other words, what adjustments did you make in your life in response to that event or pattern of events?

8. Did you "make a vow" in response to that event?

9. Did you ask God what He wanted you to do or did you begin living your life according to your wisdom?

10. Did your faith grow stronger or weaker as a result of your choice?

11. Have you asked God to show you this event or pattern of events from His perspective? What did you feel He was telling you about it?

12. If you chose your way of dealing with the situation, have you asked God to forgive you, and have you told Him you want to start handling it His way from this point forward? (If not, would you like to pray now?)

13. What is the best way for me to help you?

14. If I notice an area in your life where I think you are not totally free, do you want me to point it out to you?

Ask God to help you resolve any problem areas.

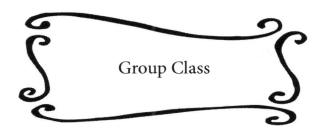

Group Class

1. What did you learn about the power of speaking to your spouse's heart that you can share with others?

2. What were some of the obstacles you ran into while attempting to speak to each other's heart?

3. Did you have any breakthroughs you would like to share with the group?

4. How did you put the steps/information into practice this week?

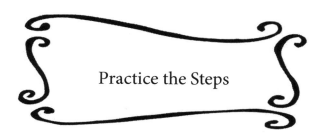

Practice the Steps

What are the next steps you need to take? List them here.

1. What is the most important change you need to make in your marriage?

2. What is the next marriage habit you want to implement? How will you implement it?

3. _____

4. _____

The Winning Couple

Chapter 11, pages 152-163 from *The Marriage Dance*
For a better understanding of this topic, we suggest you read the full chapter.

What does it take to be a "winning couple"? In dance competitions, the winning couples have invested time, money, and sweat to take dance classes. They've practiced the steps and honed their skills with private lessons. They've bought the shoes, costumes, and accessories to make their routines shine.

Contrast the couple who takes a few lessons here or there and doesn't bother to practice what they've learned. They never master the form or the steps. Their muscles aren't toned and strong. They don't improve individually—much less as a team. Instead of gliding across the floor, they pull at each other, struggling and straining, stepping on each other's toes.

Stepping on each other's toes is not the way to win the dance trophy. You can imagine what that looks like on the dance floor, but consider what it looks like in marriage. We do it frequently in marriage when both partners land on each other's pain point at the same time. Suppose a husband grows up in a family that puts a high value on being on time and a wife grows up in a family that never has time to listen to her. If he feels the need to rush out the door to be on time while she is trying to tell him something, he will hurt her feelings. At the same time, if she pressures him to hear her out, he will be frustrated. They are "stepping on each other's toes."

Take the Log Out First
Matthew 7:3-5 tells us to take the log out of our eye first so that we can see more clearly before taking the speck out of the other person's eye—in this case, our spouse. Take

your problem to the Lord and attempt to resolve it, then offer to help your spouse take a look at his or her problem. Replace the frustration with an attitude of love and service. Marriage is about character development. Grow up yourself and then you will see clearly how to help your mate.

Being a winning couple comes down to this: How much effort are you willing to put into your marriage? Do you merely want to get out on the floor and not humiliate yourself, or do you want to really dance? You can learn the steps and techniques and execute them, or you can invest yourself until you forget about the steps and techniques and enjoy dancing.

You may never do the perfect marriage dance, but you can keep improving. An infinite God always has an increasingly better marriage in store for you. As your marriage improves and continues to get better, you will inspire others that marriage has many benefits. Learning to be inter-relational and interdependent takes time and effort, but the maturity and fulfillment are worth the effort.

Improve Your Technique

"Now for this very reason also, applying all diligence, in your faith supply moral excellence, and in your moral excellence, knowledge, and in your knowledge, self-control, and in your self-control, perseverance, and in your perseverance, godliness, and in your godliness, brotherly kindness, and in your brotherly kindness, love." 2 Peter 1:5-7

In the first column, write how these verses apply to your relationship with God. In the second column, write how these verses apply to your relationship with your spouse?

Relationship with God	Relationship with Spouse

In the first column, write what impediments still prevent a happy marriage for you? In the second column, list the steps you need to take?

Impediments	Steps

Answer these personal questions.

1. Am I willing to be diligent to remove the stumbling blocks in my marriage?

2. Will I be a faithful, loving ally as my spouse works through resolving his or her sins and wounds?

3. On a scale of 1 to 10, with 10 being the best you have witnessed, rate your marriage as it is currently. Where does it need to be for you to be satisfied with it? Do you believe improvement can happen? Are you willing to do whatever is necessary to get it there?

Pray this prayer.

> "Lord, do I have sins that create walls and destroy closeness between my spouse and me? Do these walls get in the way of us coming together as You want us to?"

Answer these questions.

Am I willing to spend the time and energy and whatever else it takes (a weekly date, time together each night, a weekend marriage conference, counseling) to engage my spouse's heart and speak to his or her heart at a deeper level? How will I implement a plan to set aside this time?

Personal Questions for Men

Am I, as a husband, willing to step forward and lead my family—even when it means bucking the culture?

Even when I'm afraid and I feel as though I don't know what I'm doing, do I have the courage to get out on the "dance floor" and try?

When I feel resistance from my wife, am I willing to ask the Lord, myself, and my wife if I am leading as clearly and as gently as Jesus would?

Am I putting the needs of my partner first?

Personal Questions For Women

Am I willing to use all of my gifts and insights for the good of the team?

Am I, as a wife, willing to "stay in the arm" and let my husband lead even when I don't agree?

Am I willing to keep supporting and encouraging him even when he fails?

When I point out my husband's blind spots, am I willing to do it with gentleness and respect?

Ultimately, am I willing to put myself in God's hands and trust Him for the outcome?

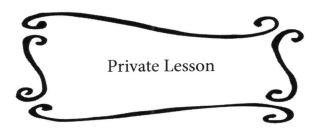

Private Lesson

Ask God to direct your discussion to the areas and issues you need to discuss.

In what areas do we step on each other's toes?

How can you join forces to help each other go through the steps?

How can the two of us – as "one flesh" – move together as one? Give at least one specific example.

Are we committed to pursuing spiritual maturity? How will we make this a priority in our marriage?

Ask God to help you resolve any problem areas.

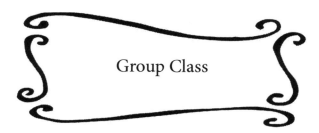

Group Class

1. What are some ways a couple can invest in their marriage?

2. Can you share an example of how a couple can "step on each other's toes?"

3. Will your willingness to love and serve your spouse and work on your personal issues first affect your spouse's response if you point out his or her blind-spot? How?

4. Share an example of how you are becoming a "winning couple."

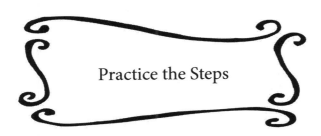

Practice the Steps

1. This week I will strengthen my marriage by giving priority to
_____.

2. This month I will strengthen my marriage by giving priority to
_____.

3. This year I will strengthen my marriage by giving priority to
_____.

Session 12

The Ultimate Marriage Dance

Chapter 12, pages 164-173 from *The Marriage Dance*
For a better understanding of this topic, we suggest you read the full chapter.

"Wives, be subject to your own husbands, as to the Lord. For the husband is the head of the wife, as Christ also is the head of the church. He Himself being the Savior of the body. But as the church is subject to Christ, so also the wives ought to be to their husbands in everything. Husbands, love your wives, just as Christ also loved the church and gave Himself up for her, so that He might sanctify her, having cleansed her by the washing of water with the word, that He might present to Himself the church in all her glory, having no spot or wrinkle or any such thing; but that she would be holy and blameless. So husbands ought also to love their own wives as their own bodies. He who loves his own wife loves himself; for no one ever hated his own flesh, but nourishes and cherishes it, just as Christ also does the church, because we are members of His body. For this reason a man shall leave his father and mother and shall be joined to his wife, and the two shall become one flesh. ***This mystery is great; but I am speaking with reference to Christ and the church.*** Nevertheless, each individual among you also is to love his own wife even as himself, and the wife must see to it that she respects her husband." Ephesians 5:22-33 [emphasis added]

A God-designed marriage is like the relationship Christ wants with His church.

Just as we use dance as an analogy for marriage, God uses marriage as an analogy for the relationship He wants with you. This marriage analogy appears throughout both the Old and New Testaments.

John 3:16 tells us God loved us so much He gave His Son to die in our place so we could have an everlasting relationship with Him.

Revelation 19:7-8 describes the uniting of Christ with His Bride at a marriage feast.

Song of Solomon is a picture of Solomon and his bride, but it can also be interpreted as a picture of the relationship God wants with us.

Isaiah 62:5 describes God rejoicing over us the way a bridegroom rejoices over his bride.

In Psalm 42:1, 63:1 & 8 and Psalm 84:2, David describes the deep, fulfilling relationship he desires with God.

Sometimes, we turn our backs on God. God describes these painful times in numerous places in the Scripture.

In Hosea 3, the reason God tells Hosea to marry a prostitute is to show Israel they were acting like adulterous wives when they pursued other gods. Instead of responding to a loving husband. Gomer, the prostitute, was chasing after other lovers.

In Isaiah 44:9-20, Psalm 115:4-8, and Jeremiah 10:3-16, God talks about the inferiority of other gods to Himself and the stupidity of chasing after them.

The worship of the Golden Calf in Exodus 32 after God had just delivered Israel by many miracles is an example of this insanity. In essence, Israel was cheating on the husband she had committed to.

God drives the same point home in Ezekiel 16 and Jeremiah 3.

The New Testament uses the same analogy.

In Matthew 22:1-14, the King invites guests to his son's wedding, but the guests reject the invitation.

In Matthew 25:1-13, Jesus tells of foolish virgins who were not ready for the bridegroom and his wedding.

Other passages—while not using the marriage analogy—describe the result of an emotionally close relationship with Christ.

John 15 tells us that a close relationship with Him brings forth fruit even as the "fruit" of a marriage relationship is new life.

Paul says his relationship with Christ is so valuable that everything he has lost is rubbish in comparison to gaining Christ (Philippians 3:8-10).

Christians throughout history also wrote about the unparalleled value of a close relationship with Christ.

Augustine said, "Thou has made us for thyself, O Lord, and our hearts are restless until they find their rest in thee."

The Westminster Shorter Catechism proclaimed, "Man's chief end is to glorify God, and to enjoy him forever."

Pascal wrote, "What else does this craving, and this helplessness, proclaim but that there was once in man a true happiness, of which all that now remains is the empty print and trace? This he tries in vain to fill with everything around him, seeking in things that are not there the help he cannot find in those that are, though none can help, since this infinite abyss can be filled only with an infinite and immutable object; in other words, by God himself."

Other religions can't claim a god with whom you can have a relationship. The god of Hinduism is in everything, and everything is god. But he is impersonal. Allah is an austere god who does not let you know whether he forgives you or not. Buddhism offers enlightenment, but not a relationship with the Almighty. Modern society substitutes science for god. There can be no relationship. In animism, you can appease and worship the gods, but not have relationship with them. Jesus stands in stark contrast. He initiates. He pursues us. He offers deep, emotional relationship.

Why does God care about having a relationship with us? First, he enjoys our voluntary worship and thanksgiving for all He has done. Second, he enjoys transforming us and making us fruitful. Third, God is love, and the essence of love is giving to others. He wants to show His love to those who are willing to respond to it. He kindly and patiently keeps inviting us into a relationship of love and joy and peace with Him. Fourth, God takes pleasure in our faith in Him as Jesus did with the centurion's faith in Luke 7:1-10. Finally, God enjoys humans telling their story of what He has done for them.

What do we receive? We receive eternal life, the ability to know and enjoy God forever, forgiveness from sins, the Holy Spirit, Christ in us, purpose in life, a new family, and power to live life as it was designed to name just a few gifts.

Many Christians don't pursue a deeper relationship with Christ because they feel their relationship is fine. Their attitude is similar to the attitude of the Church of Laodicea in Revelation 3:14-22. John said their deeds were lukewarm—mediocre—fine. As a result, Christ wants to spit them out of His mouth. But Jesus keeps calling them into deeper relationship. Pay special attention to Revelation 3:20. Jesus says he is standing at the door and knocking. If they'll only open the door, He wants to come in and share a meal with them. It is an invitation to a deep relationship with Him.

Some don't seek a deeper relationship with Christ because they are distracted by busyness—kids, jobs, debts—the worries of the world and the deceitfulness of riches. They were in love once, but they have lost their first love.

Others feel God has let them down. They feel He abandoned them or didn't change the situation when He could have. As a result, they hold God at arm's distance.

Finally, some of us simply don't like relinquishing control as a good wife or follower would. We want to do it our way.

Christ is holding out his hand and inviting you into a deeper relationship with Him. He asks to dance with you. Many have spurned God's offer. A few have accepted. What's your answer?

Read Ephesians 5:22-33. Did Paul change subjects between verse 31 and verse 32? How do you know?

What is the mega-mystery in verse 32?

Do you believe God wants a deep relationship with you? Do you want one with Him?

The verses below describe how King David sees his relationship with God. Look up the verses and rewrite them in your words.

Psalm 42:1

Psalm 63:1, 8

Psalm 84:2

Nevertheless, we sometimes reject the relationship God offers us and chase after other gods. What are the other "gods" or things you chase after rather giving priority to God?

Read John 15:4-5. Do an inventory of your life? What fruit are you producing?

Refer to the quotes from Christian writers in the first paragraphs of this section.

Would you say you worship God from the heart?

How has God transformed your life?

How have you responded to God's love?

When have you shown God your love through your faith?

Do you enjoy telling others about your love for God?

Do you think your relationship with God is good enough?

Read Revelation 3:14-22. How would you describe your relationship with Christ — cold, lukewarm, or sizzling?

What keeps you from having a better relationship with Him?

Revelation 19:7-9 is known as "The Marriage Feast of the Lamb." Why is that event given that name?

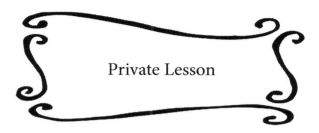

Private Lesson

Ask God to direct your discussion to the areas and issues you need to discuss.

Is our marriage showing the world a picture of the relationship Christ wants with His Bride? If so, how? If not, what can we do?

How does our marriage need to change for it to be a picture of Christ and His Bride?

If our marriage showed the world a picture of the God-man relationship, how might that give us opportunities to talk to non-believers?

Ask God to help you resolve any problem areas.

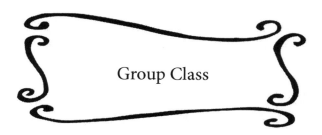

Group Class

1. Read Hosea 3, how was Israel like a prostitute? Do you think we do the same thing? How?

2. What are some of the false gods we worship? How do we cheat on God? John Eldredge calls them "less-wild lovers." Do you agree? Explain.

3. What caught your attention?

4. What did you learn?

5. What did you realize you need to be practicing?

6. How did you put the steps/information into practice this week?

7. Can your marriage be used as a tool for evangelism? How?

Practice the Steps

1. Ask God to show you the areas in which you are lukewarm.

2. Ask God to show you areas where the cares of the world restrain your relationship with Him.

3. Ask God to show you where the deceitfulness of riches has choked your testimony.

4. Ask God to show you the fruit you have produced.

5. _____

6. _____

LEADER'S GUIDE

Administration

Decide how many weeks you will use for the study. The workbook is written in 12 sessions. The sections on sins and wounds will benefit from additional time, prayer, and discussion.

Suggested 12-Week Schedule

DATE	WORKBOOK SESSION	*THE MARRIAGE DANCE* CHAPTER COVERED IN THE SESSION
	1	1~Metaphor of The Marriage Dance 2~Embrace Your Differences
	2	3~Do You Want to Dance? 4~Connect the Partners
	3	5~Lead with Confidence
	4	6~Follow with Strength
	5	7A~Sins (Bitterness)
	6	7B~Sins (Pride)
	7	7C~Sins (Rebellion, Craving Things that Don't Last, Sexual Sins, Hypocrisy)
	8	8~Wounds: Everyone is Wounded
	9	9~Wounds: Beware Your Reaction
	10	10~Wounds: Resolution of Wounds
	10 Bonus	Bonus~Help Your Partner Resolve His or Her Wounds
	11	11~The Winning Couple
	12	12~The Ultimate Marriage Dance

An alternate 8-week schedule might look like this:

Date	
	Sessions 1
	Session 2
	Sessions 3 and 4
	Sessions 5 and 6
	Session 7
	Sessions 8 and 9
	Session 10
	Session 11 and 12

If scheduling does not permit 8 or 12 weeks in a row, the study can be broken into three mini-studies with at least one week dedicated to each session.

Date	Mini-Study	Covers workbook sessions:
	Emotional Intimacy	2, 11, 12
	Lead with Confidence – Follow with Strength	1, 3, 4
	Removing Relational Roadblocks	5, 6, 7, 8, 9, 10 + Bonus

If you can spend more time on Sins and Wounds, do it. A 16-week Schedule might look like this:

Date	WORKBOOK SESSION
	Session 1
	Session 2
	Session 3
	Session 4
	Session 5—Bitterness
	Session 6—Pride
	Session 7—Rebellion, Craving Things that Don't Last

	Session 7—Sexual Sins, Hypocrisy
	Session 8
	Session 9
	Session 9
	Session 10
	Session 10
	Bonus Session
	Session 11
	Session 12

Administrative Decisions to Make Before you Begin

1. Will the study take place at church, in a home, or _____? Consider your best option for making the setting relaxed and comfortable.

2. Reserve your times on the church calendar, home, or other location. As a rule, avoid the holiday season and summer vacations.

3. Childcare: Will there be childcare? How will you handle it? Will it be free or is there a cost? We recommend hiring a childcare worker if you cannot find a volunteer. If you are encouraging younger participants to come, this is crucial.

4. Promotion: Schedule bulletin, website, live, audio/visual, and social media announcements.

5. How will sign-ups be taken?

6. Is there a cost for the study? Will the church underwrite the cost of the books and childcare or will participants pay the cost? Couples are more committed if they pay at least part of the cost themselves.

7. Order books. *The Marriage Dance: Moving Together as One* and *The Marriage Dance: Practice the Steps* (workbook), both by Bob and Roxann Andersen are available at www.Amazon.com.

Schedule

Prepare a handout for participants detailing the date each session in the workbook will be covered and the corresponding chapters they should read in *The Marriage Dance*.

Forms

Roll /Attendance. Prepare a roll sheet which lists name, phone number, email address, and the days each participant attends. Take attendance. Call anyone who misses a session.

Leader or Lead Couple

If you are going through this workbook with a group, it is best to have a lead couple. The lead couple opens the group in prayer. They have read the chapter of *The Marriage Dance* that will be covered each week and they take the group through a review of the principles that were covered. When possible, they should substitute a personal story that illustrates the point instead of using the authors' stories. This will make your study more personable.

We recommend you do not have the lead couple double as a mentor couple (below) or facilitator if possible. This allows them to host an "open table" for people who might drop in. It is best not to put a new person or couple into a group after the first couple of weeks. You are fostering an atmosphere of safety and forming trust between couples. Groups may become reluctant to share if you add a new couple to an established group. In addition, the lead couple may need to perform certain administrative tasks during the group discussion or be free to answer questions or deal with a couple who would benefit from a one-on-one conversation.

Intercessory Prayer Team

Consider enlisting prayer warriors who will pray for each couple during the course of the study.

Mentor Couples

We highly recommend the incorporation of mentor couples. They serve as a loving, godly presence for the couples in the group. They provide a safe place if a couple has something they don't feel they can share within the group.

We recommend asking mentor couples to serve rather than issuing a blanket invitation to volunteer. Look for these qualifications in a mentor couple:

- A couple who has been married at least 10 years and are happy with each other.

- A couple who is wise, safe, listens well, encouraging, seasoned. Someone who can build rapport with their "mentees." Human, honest, mature. *They know they are not perfect.* Objective and impartial. Reassuring. Willing to share their life experiences—including their struggles—and how they resolved the problem. Willing to model what a godly marriage looks like.

- A couple who knows how to deal with conflict, stress, and crisis and are willing to share how they overcame these experiences to create an enjoyable marriage.

- A couple who is able and willing to answer questions.

- A couple that loves and respects one another. They share emotional, spiritual, and physical intimacy. You can tell they enjoy being together.

- A couple does not need to be trained counselors. They are fellow "dancers" with more experience.

- A couple with a heart's desire to help marriages.

- A couple who is willing to meet with other couples or their group outside of the specified meeting time.

- A couple who will commit to being present for the entire workshop unless there is an emergency.

- A couple who will pray for each member of their group.

- A couple who is willing to complete 60-90 minutes of homework each week in order to prepare for the session.

- A couple who is willing to take a phone call during the week if one of the couples at their table has a question.

Marriage Ministry as Outreach

Consider using this marriage study as an opportunity to invite un-churched friends and to reach out to your community. Those who are somewhat disappointed in their marriage, feel their spouse is not treating them right, wish their mate would spend less time with work, sports, or sitting on the couch may not come to a regular church service but may accept an invitation to a discussion group about marriage. The session entitled, "The Ultimate Marriage Dance" explains the relationship Christ wants with us and can be used evangelistically. Most non-Christians want a good marriage too. As they see your group working through the same struggles they have, they may be challenged as they see the Holy Spirit transforming your lives and marriages. Who do you want to reach out to, and how will you contact them? Consider having a pastor or someone with the gift of evangelism present during "The Ultimate Marrage Dance" session.

Room Set-up

Round tables are best for group discussion. Set them far enough apart to allow each group to hear their own discussion without being distracted by neighboring groups but close enough to keep the energy of the group.

Extending the benefits of *The Marriage Dance*

How will your group continue the discussion after the study is done? Try to nurture the supportive community you've created and expand that community by:

1. Meeting once a month and picking a topic to discuss at length. You might use an entire evening to discuss one question in the workbook. The areas of sins and wounds are particularly valuable to spend additional time on. Ask your group for marriage topics they would like to discuss. Create a relaxed atmosphere. Ask participants to bring snacks.

2. Two to four times a year, have a date night or social. Be creative. Customize it to the needs and desires of your group.

3. Sign up for free weekly marriage tips at https://themarriagedance.com/contact/.

FAQs

Is the study good for pre-marrieds?

Yes! We highly recommend it. If couples can resolve their sins and wounds before marriage, they will have fewer problems after marriage.

How about singles?

Yes. Sessions 5-10 are relevant for anyone. The principles of how sins and wounds create relational roadblocks are relevant whether you are relating to your spouse, a family member, or a co-worker. Working through and resolving the roadblocks will improve all your relationships.

Do We Have to Dance?

Nothing in this study requires any couple to dance. However, dancing allows the couple to appreciate the problems of leading and following.

Resources

Read *The Marriage Dance: Moving Together as One,* by Bob and Roxann Andersen

Host *The Marriage Dance* seminar or a marriage event at your church. https://themarriagedance.com/contact/

Sign up for "Time to Make Your Marriage Dance," free weekly email tips for suggestions on how to keep improving your marriage. https://themarriagedance.com/contact/

Read the weekly blog posts on marriage at www.TheMarriageDance.com or www.Facebook.com/themarriagedance.

Made in the USA
Lexington, KY
18 September 2019